# Sons
# of
# Abraham

NINTH PRINTING

# Walter F. White

# Sons
# of
# Abraham

**Walter F. White**

ISBN 1-55630-863-9

PUBLISHED BY:
BRENTWOOD CHRISTIAN PRESS
4000 BEALLWOOD AVENUE
COLUMBUS, GEORGIA 31904

Unless Otherwise stated, all Scripture quotations are taken from the New King James Version. Copyright 1982 by Thomas Nelson Inc.

Husbands, love your wives, just as
Christ also loved the church and
gave Himself for her,
(Ephesians 5:25)

Special Recognition

To my wife Gene (Genevieve) who for forty three-years has been my companion, my friend, my lover, and my helpmate. She is in reality the "Woman of Valor", spoken of in Proverbs 31.

# Contents

| *Chapter* | *Page* |
|---|---|

Introduction................................................................7

1. The Marriage Vow ................................................11

2. Creation .................................................................15

3. The Enemy .............................................................20

4. Manhood................................................................31

5. The Heart................................................................39

6. Headship................................................................48

7. Parenting................................................................59

8. Rebellion ...............................................................70

9. Bitterness...............................................................75

10. The Tongue ..........................................................82

11. Love .....................................................................88

12. The "Be" Attitudes.............................................101

13. One Little Rose ..................................................120

14. Accountability — Responsibility — Commitment ..........125

15. Abide..................................................................131

Epilogue....................................................................148

# INTRODUCTION

In 1977, I made Jesus the Lord of my life. I invited Him into my heart and asked Him to forgive me and change me. He sure did do that! I am a totally different person than I was back then. I am doing things that I would never have dreamed of doing and never would have believed I could do...like writing a book. I am not a Bible scholar, and I am certainly not a theologian, but I want to be obedient to what I feel God has been urging me to do.

The subjects of manhood, headship, and fatherhood are complex and personal. If I were to try to answer every question about every situation and every circumstance that one might encounter, I would be taking on quite an assignment, an impossible one. I am bringing to you my thoughts and what I have learned through prayer and studying God's Word. Most of what I have to say I've learned through trial and error.

I have been married to my wife Gene, for forty-three years. We have four children and five grandchildren, and our nephew came to live with us after his mother died. As you might guess, we have had our share of challenges. I have made many errors, but, "Praise God," I have learned from them all, and I am still learning.

Quite a few years ago, my wife Gene, after studying the scriptures, began to see what was required of her as a wife and began to put the principle of submission into practice. It sounds wonderful to have a wife who is willing to submit to you, but I didn't like it. It put a tremendous amount of responsibility on me. No longer could I answer her with comments like "I don't care", or "Do whatever you want to do." Now, I not only had to take an interest in everything, but I also had to make decisions. I didn't like this kind of pressure, and I didn't want it. It was easier the other way: If I let her make the decisions and things worked out, that was fine. If they didn't work out, I could blame her.

I thought about it a lot and it seemed to me, that if she *was* right and God *did* have such clear and concise instructions for wives, then He must also have a plan for husbands, something besides working and making money. I decided to search the scriptures to see what God had to say about the man's role. The more I looked into it the more I realized that we men have a tremendous responsibility as the head of our wives and families.

*But I want you to know that, the head of every man is Christ the head of woman is man, and the head of Christ is God.*

*(1 Corinthians 11:3)*

The world has perverted manhood and we have become wimps. "Strong words," you might say, and they are, but they are true.

Television, movies, videos, magazines, etc. are having extremely negative influences on the family. The kind of man that is portrayed in this so-called entertainment medium is not the kind of man God created us to be. The idea depicted is of a man who makes a lot of money, accepts no responsibility for anything, sees nothing wrong with anything, sleeps around with everyone or anyone who gives him a second look. He smokes, drinks, and gets rid of any-one who gets in his way. In that world anyone who is decent is a wimp. Well, I would rather be a man in the eyes of God, even if it means being a wimp in the eyes of the world, because being a man in the eyes of the world is being a wimp in the eyes of God.

Who are we going to take our direction from, the world or from God?

The Bible says in 2 Timothy 3: 16-17 that:

*All Scripture is given by inspiration of God, and is **profitable** for **doctrine**, for **reproof**, for **correction**, for **instruction in righteousness**, [17] that the man of God may be complete, thoroughly equipped for every good work.*

**<u>Profitable</u>** - Advantageous, beneficial, desirable, expedient, gainful, lucrative, productive, useful.

**Doctrine** - Whatever is taught, the act of teaching, whatever is laid down as true by an instructor or master. The doctrines of the gospel are the principles or truths taught by Christ and His apostles.

**Reproof** - Blame expressed to the face; censure for a fault.

**Correction** - The act of bringing back from error.

**Instruction in righteousness** - Purity of heart, conformity of heart and life to the divine law.

Along with the scriptures we will be examining practical ways to apply what we are learning. What am I trying to accomplish? I am trying to show that we are living in a world where manhood has been perverted. Webster's definition of perverted is " to turn from the truth or from its proper purpose: to distort from its true use."

**Let us seek the truth of the Word of God, walk in obedience to it and receive the blessings of Abraham for ourselves and our families.**

*And if you are Christ's, then you are Abraham's seed, and heirs according to the promise.*
*(Galatians 3:29)*

# 1

## The Marriage Vow

"I, Walter take thee Genevieve, to be my lawfully wedded wife, to have and to hold from this day forth, and do promise ( or vow) before God and these witnesses, to love, honor, protect and keep you, for better or for worse, for richer or for poorer, in sickness and in health, and to cleave to you, and you only till death do us part, or for as long as we both shall live."

We stood before God and the witnesses that we invited to our wedding and made a vow similar to the one above. We made a vow **to** God and a covenant **to** each other to love, honor, protect and keep each other in the good times ( better) and in the bad times (worse).

A vow is a solemn promise made **to** God.

Webster's 1828 dictionary says that in a moral and religious sense, vows are promises **to** God, as they appeal **to** God to witness their sincerity and the violation of them is a most heinous ( heinous means: hateful, odious, enormous as a heinous sin or crime) offense.

How serious is God about making vows? Let us look to the scriptures to find the answer.

*... you shall not make false vows , but shall fulfill your vows to the lord.*

(Matthew 5: 33 NASB)

*Whatever your lips utter you must be sure to do, because you made your vow freely to the LORD your God with your own mouth.*

(Deuteronomy 23:23 NIV )

*Once you make the vow, you must be careful to do as you have said, for it was your own choice, and you have vowed to the lord your God.*

(Deuteronomy23:23 Living Bible)

*When you make a vow to God, do not delay in fulfilling it. He has no pleasure in fools; fulfill your vow. [5] It is better not to vow than to make a vow and not fulfill it. [6] Do not let your mouth lead you into sin. And do not protest to the temple messenger, "My vow was a mistake." Why should God be angry at what you say and destroy the work of your hands?*

(Ecclesiastes 5:4-6 NIV)

*When a man makes a vow to the LORD or takes an oath to obligate himself by a pledge, he must not break his word but must do everything he said.*

(Numbers 30:2 NIV )

Is God serious about vows? What do you think?

In Malachi 2:14 it says the Lord was a witness to the covenant made at your marriage. A covenant is a coming together — a meeting or agreement of minds.

Most couples as they are entering into marriage today are unaware of the importance of the covenant they are making with each other and the seriousness of the solemn vow they are making to God. They have no idea of what it takes to make a marriage work. They don't understand that God designed the institution of marriage, and He did not do a half-baked job. He gave the man and the woman certain roles in the marriage, and He defines these roles very clearly in His Word.

He not only designed marriage, but He also is in favor of it.

*He who finds a wife finds a good thing, And obtains favor from the LORD.*

*(Proverbs 18:22)*

Today, marriages are going bad. It seems as though people work harder at getting out of marriage than they do at making them work. God hates divorce, and it is not an alternative.

*But I say to you that whoever divorces his wife for any reason except sexual immorality causes her to commit adultery; and whoever marries a woman who is divorced commits adultery.*

*(Matthew 5:32)*

*Therefore what God has joined together, let not man separate." [10] In the house His disciples also asked Him again about the same matter. [11] So He said to them, "Whoever divorces his wife and marries another commits adultery against her. [12] And if a woman divorces her husband and marries another, she commits adultery."*

*(Mark 10:9-12)*

*For the woman who has a husband is bound by the law to her husband as long as he lives. But if the husband dies, she is released from the law of her husband.*
*(Romans 7:2)*

*Now to the married I command, yet not I but the Lord: A wife is not to depart from her husband. [11] But even if she does depart, let her remain unmarried or be reconciled to her husband. And a husband is not to divorce his wife.*
*(1 Cor. 7:10-11)*

The vows we made to each other should never be forgotten. It would be a good idea for all of us to write them out and put them in a place where they could be read and reflected on often, especially when the road gets rough, and we are feeling overwhelmed. If you don't remember the exact words you said when you made your vows, they were probably very similar to those at the beginning of this chapter.

# 2

# Creation

It is important for us to go to the book of Genesis and study a little bit about creation.

*Then God said, "Let Us make man in Our image, according to Our likeness; let them have dominion over the fish of the sea, over the birds of the air, and over the cattle, over all the earth and over every creeping thing that creeps on the earth." [27] So God created man in His own image; in the image of God He created him; male and female He created them.*

*(Genesis 1:26-27)*

Then God said, (God was having a conversation with someone and that someone could only be Jesus) "Let Us (more than one) make man in Our ( more than one) image, according to Our likeness": We are made in the image of God. What does God look like? He looks like us. (vs. 27) So God created man in His own image; in the image of God He created him; He created him male,and He created him female.

*And the LORD God formed man of the dust of the ground, and breathed into his nostrils the breath of life; and man became a living being.*

*(Genesis 2:7)*

15

Now we see how He did it. He took some dust from the ground and formed a man and breathed into his nostrils the breath of life, and man became a living being. At this point creation of the man (male and female) was completed.

Then God said, "It is not good that man should be alone. I will make him a helper comparable to him." (Genesis 2:18)

In Genesis 2: 19-20 we see God creating all the animals, birds and creatures. But for Adam there was not found a helper comparable to him.

Genesis 2: 21-25 covers the forming or making of the woman and the institution of marriage.

Genesis 2:18 Amp. " I will make him a helper (extension, completer, assistant, servant,) comparable to him (worthy of comparison, being of equal regard.)"

God had a reason why He created the woman the way that He did. He wanted somebody comparable to man **<u>but not the same.</u>** If God wanted man and woman to be equal in the sense that each one would be capable of doing whatever the other could do, if He wanted that kind of equality, all He had to do was reach down, take another handful of dust and create another person. Notice in this verse that the woman is equal to the man. In the eyes of God, she is equal, but she has a different function.

When God created man, He also created the woman. All of God's characteristics were within the man already. All He had to do was extract a portion of His nature from man and make a companion for him.

Why did God choose the rib? *The Encyclopedia Americana* defines the rib as, "the main support and protection for the lungs and the heart." The rib protects these two vital organs for without them there would be no life. I don't believe that it is a coincidence that God chose the rib. Just as the rib plays such a vital role in the protection and support of the lung and heart, the woman as the man's helper has a vital role in protecting and supporting her husband.

The woman's role in a marriage needs to be identified, understood, and respected. She was not created to be put down, nor was she created to be the head of the family.

*Then the rib which the LORD God had taken from man He made into a woman, and He brought her to the man.*

*(Genesis 2:22)*

God took the woman and brought her unto the man. God's gift to man ... woman.

Now, man's authority started in Genesis 2:19. God brought every creature to Adam, " And whatever Adam called each living creature, that was **its** name. After God brought what He had formed to the man, Adam declared, " This is now bone of my bones and flesh of my flesh; she shall be called woman (the Hebrew is Ishshah, a she man)" because she was taken out of man. Genesis 2:23

*Therefore a man shall leave his father and mother and be joined to his wife, and they shall become one flesh.*

*(Genesis 2:24)*

The two shall become one — singular in number. Nothing on earth is meant to be as close as the relationship between a husband and a wife. It is comparable to the relationship between the Father, the Son, and the Holy Spirit. They are one. Even though they are three different persons with unique functions, they are still one. A husband and his wife, even though they each have their own minds, their own spirits, their own roles, they are still one. "For this reason a man shall leave his father and mother and shall be united firmly ( joined inseparably ) to his wife and the two shall become one flesh." (Matthew 19:25 Amp.)

The more we dig into and study God's Word, the more we will see that everything did not just happen by chance. **God had and still has a plan.**

We know that from the time of Adam right up to the time of Jesus, man sought a way back to God.

but there was no way. So God sent His Son into the world so that we would have a way back to Him.

God has built into man a natural desire to seek Him and to know Him.

> *"But God shows His anger from heaven against all sinful, evil men who push away the truth from them. **For the truth about God is known to them instinctively; God has put this knowledge in their hearts.** Since earliest times men have seen the earth and sky and all God made and have known of His existence, and great eternal power, so they will have no excuse [when they stand before God at Judgment Day]."*
>
> *(Romans 1:18-20 Living Bible)*

Man has always thought he could be fulfilled by: Women — Money — Power. In his pursuit of happiness he has been greatly influenced by these three forces. The course of history has been changed by these influences. The only real fulfillment is found in **Jesus Christ.**

# 3

# The Enemy

*Now the serpent was more cunning than any beast of the field which the LORD God had made. And he said to the woman, "Has God indeed said, 'You shall not eat of every tree of the garden'?" [2] And the woman said to the serpent, "We may eat the fruit of the trees of the garden; [3] but of the fruit of the tree which is in the midst of the garden, God has said, 'You shall not eat it, nor shall you touch it, lest you die.' " [4] Then the serpent said to the woman, "You will not surely die. [5] For God knows that in the day you eat of it your eyes will be opened, and you will be like God, knowing good and evil." [6] So when the woman saw that the tree was good for food, that it was pleasant to the eyes, and a tree desirable to make one wise, she took of its fruit and ate. She also gave to her husband with her, and he ate. [7] Then the eyes of both of them were opened, and they knew that they were naked; and they sewed fig leaves together and made themselves coverings. [8] And they heard the sound of the LORD God walking in the garden in the cool of the day, and Adam and his wife hid themselves from the presence of the LORD God among the trees of the garden.*

*[9] Then the LORD God called to Adam and said*

*to him, "Where are you?" [10] So he said, "I heard Your voice in the garden, and I was afraid because I was naked; and I hid myself." [11] And He said, "Who told you that you were naked? Have you eaten from the tree of which I commanded you that you should not eat?" [12] Then the man said, "The woman whom You gave to be with me, she gave me of the tree, and I ate."*

*(Genesis 3:1-12)*

Genesis 3:1 " Now the serpent was more cunning than any beast of the field which the Lord God had made." He was a deceiver, a cheater, a liar back then, and he still is today. He wants to pull us as far away from God as he can, and he will do everything he can to destroy us.

*The thief does not come except to steal, and to kill, and to destroy.*

*(John 10:10)*

We read further in Geneses 3:1 "And he said to the woman. 'Has God indeed said, you shall not eat of every tree of the garden'?" If we examine this question, we will see how devious it was. It was not a threatening question. It was harmless. The serpent appeared to want to know more about God's Word. The woman innocently answered him although she added to what God had said. It appears that after communicating with the serpent,

Eve was convinced that eating of the fruit would make their already-perfect life even better.

The serpent knew he couldn't deceive Adam so he went to the weaker vessel.

*Husbands, likewise, dwell with them with under-standing, giving honor to the wife, as to the weaker vessel, ...*

*(1Peter 3:7)*

He needed to trick her into usurping man's divinely appointed position. Actually, the serpent was under the control and dominion of the woman already. (Genesis 1:26) She did not need to answer him. All she had to do was send him to her husband, Adam. Interesting! The woman was deceived, by the serpent. The man was tempted, by the woman.

In Genesis 3:12 we get our first glimpse of man's wimpy nature. Adam said to God, " The woman whom you gave to be with me, she gave me of the tree, and I ate." Notice that when the punishments were given out, God was angry with Adam FIRST because he listened to his wife, THEN because he ate from the tree.

*Then to Adam He said, "Because you have heeded the voice of your wife, and have eaten from the tree of which I commanded you, saying, 'You shall not eat of it':*

*(Genesis 3:17)*

22

God didn't listen to man's excuses back then, and He's not going to listen to our excuses when we stand before Him to give an account of our headship.

*I, therefore, the prisoner of the Lord, beseech you to walk worthy of the calling with which you were called.*
*(Ephesians 4:1)*

God has a purpose for our lives. Every man has a calling and is expected to live out his role. We are called to be the heads of our families.

*But I want you to know that the head of every man is Christ, the head of woman is man, and the head of Christ is God.*

*(1 Corinthians 11:3)*

*For the husband is head of the wife, as also Christ is head of the church; and He is the Savior of the body.*
*(Ephesians 5:23)*

As the heads of our families, we are the ones who should be fighting off the schemes of the enemy. I often wonder what would have happened if when Eve brought the fruit to Adam, he had said, " NO, God has commanded me not to eat of that tree and I will not, and as your head I am telling you, put that fruit down." He didn't do that. What he did do was allow himself to be talked in to doing something that he knew was wrong. Adam listened to his wife and gave in to temptation. Now am I saying we are not to listen to our wives? No, I am not saying that at all! My wife is my help-mate and my best friend. I prayerfully listen to everything she has to say. But we must be sober and vigilant because our adversary will try to destroy us any way he can. He used Eve to get to Adam, and he will try to use our wives to get to us. Recognize that God said " I will put enmity (ill-will, hatred) between thee (Satan) and the woman."(Genesis3:15)

A woman's role is to submit to her husband. "To Submit" means "to surrender a person's will and power to the control or government of another" (Webster's 1828), a very difficult thing to do, especially if you have been going the world's way. Most women cringe at the word "submit". They think they need a 50/50 arrangement in every area of the marriage to fulfill their roles. Most of the time, they are sincere, but they are sincerely wrong. They have been deceived. When they begin to understand their God - given role, it is difficult for them. It is a real wrenching experience to give up the old ideas and habits. It takes a real willingness to die to self, to submit to another's authority and to take on the role of "helper" and "supporter", especially when you consider yourself a partner. When you have a partnership, you have two heads, and two heads, we know makes a monster. When a decision needs to be made and each party has a different opinion, one has to give in, and very often that can cause bad feelings and dissension. Understanding the principles of authority and submission will help a couple break away from 50/50 thinking.

A man learns his role and is promoted into headship. A woman learns her role and is brought into submission. She is not going to find this easy. The first, and the hardest thing she has to learn is to distinguish between true submission "as unto the Lord" and false submission which is "unto her husband." False submission is when women submit with wrong motives. A woman literally has to be willing to allow the Lord to reshape and remold her into a new woman in order for her to submit.

*You married women, be submissive to your own husbands (subordinate yourselves as being secondary to and dependent on them, and adapt yourselves to them), so that even if any do not obey the Word (of God), they may be won over not by discussion but by the (Godly) lives of their wives. When they observe the pure and modest way in which you conduct yourselves. Together with your reverence (for your husband; you are to feel for him all that reverence includes; to respect, defer to, revere him — to honor, esteem, appreciate, prize, and, in the human sense, to adore him, that is, to admire, praise, be devoted to, deeply love, and enjoy your husband).*

*(1 Peter 3:1-2 Amplified Bible)*

A woman has to truly desire to be obedient to God, to be willing to put herself through the pain of making these adjustments. Submission requires her to examine her heart. It requires her to deal with the attitudes of rebellion and resentment that she has held towards her husband and towards God.

On the positive side, once she begins to understand her role, and lives it, she experiences true liberation. God can really do a work in a woman who submits and yields herself to the Lord. The combination of a husband who is the head according to God's Word and a wife who is in submission to him, according to God's Word is unbeatable and makes for a heaven on earth marriage and relationship.

We, as husbands and the heads of our wives, are to guide and guard them through any and all of the tough times that they might be experiencing. We have been designated to be their covering and we should be taking authority over the principalities and powers of darkness that come against our wives. We should be rebuking them in the name of Jesus.

*So then each of us shall give account of himself to God.*
*(Romans 14:12)*

*O Timothy! Guard what was committed to your trust.*
*(1 Timothy 6:20)*

Yes Timothy! Guard what was committed to your trust. We will be called to give an account to God for the things that have been committed to our trust. Our wives have been committed to **our** trust. <u>**We must guard them.**</u>

In the scripture we never read of the women going to war or fighting the battles, always the men. We must fight for our wives, our sons and daughters, our grandchildren, our homes, our churches, our neighborhoods. We must defend them against the wiles of the enemy.

The question is: How do we battle a foe who is so much more powerful than we are? One who is deceitful, one who lies and cheats and steals, one who we cannot see? The answer is that in the flesh we cannot fight and beat such a foe. But, because of the power and authority we have in the name of the One who is in us, we have dominion over the enemy.

*You are of God, little children, and have overcome them, because He who is in you is greater than he who is in the world.*

*(1 John 4:4)*

*Behold, I give you the authority to trample on serpents and scorpions, and over all the power of the enemy, and nothing shall by any means hurt you.*
*(Luke 10:19 )*

The enemy will do everything he can to destroy us, to bring us down, to discourage us, and to pull us away from the Lord. He knows our weaknesses because most of us are confessing them all the time.

What are we to do? The scripture clearly tells us:

1) <u>Put</u> on the whole armor of God.

*Put on the whole armor of God, that you may be able to stand against the wiles of the devil. [12] For we do not wrestle against flesh and blood, but against principalities, against powers, against the rulers of the darkness of this age, against spiritual hosts of wickedness in the heavenly places. [13] Therefore take up the whole armor of God, that you may be able to withstand in the evil day, and having done all, to stand. [14] Stand therefore, having girded your waist with truth, having put on the breastplate of righteousness, [15] and having shod your feet with the preparation of the gospel of peace; [16] above all, taking the shield of faith with which you will be able to quench all the fiery darts of the wicked one.*

*Ephesians 6:11-16)*

(2) <u>Use</u> the weapons of our warfare.

*For the weapons of our warfare are not carnal but mighty in God for pulling down strongholds,*

*(2 Corinthians 10:4)*

The only weapons that are adequate enough to destroy the fortresses of Satan are those that come from God. You cannot fight him with carnal weapons, that is: strength, talents, wealth, ingenuity, psychology or philosophy.

The enemy cannot stand against the armor of God or the weapons of God's warfare. He has to give up!

These are the mighty weapons of God that we are instructed to use against the enemy to pull down the strongholds and protect our wives, our families, and all that concerns us.

### (1) **The Word:**

*And take the helmet of salvation, and the sword of the Spirit, which is the word of God;*

*(Ephesians 6:17)*

### (2) **The Name:**

*And these signs will follow those who believe: In My name they will cast out demons; they will speak with new tongues; [18] they will take up serpents; and if they drink anything deadly, it will by no means hurt them; they will lay hands on the sick, and they will recover."*

*(Mark 16:17-18)*

### (3) **The Blood:**

*And they overcame him by the blood of the Lamb and by the word of their testimony, and they did not love their lives to the death.*

*(Revelation 12:11)*

We have been given the weapons, but we fail to use them. We look to the world first for our answers, and as a last resort, we look to God. The answers to all problems are found in the Word, in His Name, and in His Blood.

# 4

# Manhood

Webster's 1828 Dictionary defines manhood as:

1. The state of one who is a **man**, of an adult male, or one who is advanced beyond puberty, boyhood or childhood.
2. Virility, as opposed to womanhood.
3  Human nature, as the manhood of Christ.
4. The qualities of a man, courage, bravery.

Because we were born a male does that make us a man?

Webster defines male as:
1. Pertaining to the sex that procreates young, and applied to animals of all kinds; as a male child; a male beast, fish or fowl.

2. Denoting the sex of a plant which produces the fecundating dust, or a flower or plant that bears the stamens only, without pistils. Denoting the screw whose threads enter the grooves or channels of the corresponding or female screw.

Being born a male does not make us a man. God Himself is the One who gave us the name "man." Then God said, "Let us make man in Our image, according to, Our likeness" (Genesis 1:26). So then a man is someone who has the nature and characteristics of God, and manhood is the state of being a man. When God sent His Son into the world, He was saying to us, " This is what I want man to be like, this is My idea of a real man."

The world has perverted man and manhood. To live in the world today and to be a man in the eyes of God, **takes courage.** This involves change, and it takes courage to change. This change will not be easy because it means looking deep into our own hearts and saying, " Lord change me!"

The prophet Joel said,

> So rend your heart, and not your garments; Return to the LORD your God.
>
> (Joel 2:13)

"To rend" means: "To separate any substance into parts with force or sudden violence; to tear asunder; to split."(Webster's 1828)

Oh! We can find a lot of excuses for the way we are. We can blame people, our fathers, mothers, wives, children, our ministers, priests, pastors. But are we willing to look into our own hearts, and yes, even rend them if necessary? Are we willing to say to God: **Make me a man**, in your Image and Likeness? **Make me a husband**, who loves,

32

leads and protects, as Jesus loves, leads and protects His church. **Make me a father**, like you. A father who will teach, train, provide for, nurture, control, and most importantly *love*. We as men, have an awesome responsibility to fulfill the role that God has designed for us.

To walk in the fullness of God is so much better than anything one can receive from the world. The man who finds life will find it through trusting in God.

2 Cor. 5:17 says;

*Therefore, if anyone is in Christ, he is a new creation; old things have passed away; behold, all things have become new.*

When we become born again, we become new creatures. The "new creature" to whom Paul is referring is the inward man. In order to understand this better, look at 2 Corinthians 4:16;

*Therefore we do not lose heart. Even though our outward man is perishing, yet the inward man is being renewed day by day.*

That means the sin nature in our spirit has been done away with. It's gone. The inward man has taken on a new nature, the nature of God. The more we renew the inward man, the more Christlike we become. The sins that plague the outward man begin to vanish. Even as Christians we will always have the flesh to deal with, and we will have to keep it under the dominion of our spirit. We have to crucify the flesh.

*But I discipline my body and bring it into subjection, lest, when I have preached to others, I myself should become disqualified.*

*(1 Corinthians 9:27)*

We must bring the flesh under subjection. It hurts, but we must present our bodies to God as a living sacrifice.

*I beseech you therefore, brethren, by the mercies of God, that you present your bodies a living sacrifice, holy, acceptable to God, which is your reasonable service. [2] And do not be conformed to this world, but be transformed by the renewing of your mind, that you may prove what is that good and acceptable and perfect will of God.*

*(Romans 12:1-2)*

God speaks to us through our spirit. His Spirit communicates with our spirit (our born again spirit). But this will occur only when we are in union with Him, when we take time to be with Him, and we put Him first in everything in our lives. We have a choice to make. Which way are we going to go? We've been given a free will to make the choice. Will it be God's way or the world's way?

*"See, I have set before you today life and good, death and evil, [16] in that I command you today to love the LORD your God, to walk in His ways, and to keep His commandments, His statutes, and His judgments, that you may live and multiply; and the LORD your God will bless you in the land which you go to possess. [17] But if your heart turns away so that you do not hear, and are drawn away, and worship other gods and serve them, [18] I announce to you today that you shall surely perish; you shall not prolong your days in the land which you cross over the Jordan to go in and possess. [19] I call heaven and earth as witnesses today against you, that I have set before you life and death, blessing and cursing; **therefore choose life**, that both you and your descendants may live;*
*(Deuteronomy 30:15-19)*

## The world is the product of worldly wisdom.

*Who is wise and understanding among you? Let him show by good conduct that his works are done in the meekness of wisdom. [14] But if you have bitter envy and self-seeking in your hearts, do not boast and lie against the truth. [15] This wisdom does not descend from above, but is earthly, sensual, demonic. [16] **For where envy and self-seeking exist, confusion and every evil thing are there.***
*(James 3:13-16)*

We need wisdom, but we need God's wisdom, the wisdom from above.

*But the wisdom that is from above is first pure, then peaceable, gentle, willing to yield, full of mercy and good fruits, without partiality and without hypocrisy.*

*(James 3:17)*

We **cannot** look to the world for a definition of our manhood; we **cannot** look to the world for our example of how a husband should act; we **cannot** look to the world to receive our direction for our fatherhood. We **must** look to the Word of God.

Unless we understand our roles, and our wives understand their roles, and we understand each others' roles we will not be able to function properly in them. At the same time, if we have a wife who is unsaved, or even saved but rebellious, we cannot use her lack of co-operation as an excuse for our disobedience to God. Unless we know the source of our knowledge and seek after Him, we will never be the man God wants us to be, and furthermore, we will miss our blessings. We must realize that we too can perish for lack of knowledge.

*My people are destroyed for lack of knowledge.*
*(Hosea 4:6)*

A mixture of the wisdom and the ways of God with the wisdom and the ways of the world will not work for you. You will end up with religion or with what I have heard called, Pious Mish-Mosh !

The highest example of manhood is "Jesus Christ."

*For whom He foreknew, He also predestined to be conformed to the image of His Son, that He might be the firstborn among many brethren*
*(Romans 8:29)*

Jesus is the firstborn. It is the "many brethren" that He is looking for. Manhood and Christlikeness go hand and hand. **The highest measure of manhood is to be like Jesus.** He is a perfect man in every way. If we are going to have a hero, an idol, or a role model, make it Jesus Christ. **You can't go wrong !**

Some might say, " But Jesus never married." True ! Jesus didn't marry the way that we do, but he does have a bride (the body of Christ) the Church.

*For as a young man marries a virgin, So shall your sons marry you; And as the bridegroom rejoices over the bride, So shall your God rejoice over you.*
*(Isaiah 62:5)*

*For I am jealous for you with godly jealousy. For I have betrothed you to one husband, that I may present you as a chaste virgin to Christ.*
*(2 Corinthians 11:2)*

*Let us be glad and rejoice and give Him glory, for the marriage of the Lamb has come, and His wife has made herself ready."*
*(Revelation 19:7)*

*And the Spirit and the bride say, "Come!" And let him who hears say, "Come!" And let him who thirsts come. Whoever desires, let him take the water of life freely.*

*(Revelation 22:17)*

He wants our marriages to be patterned after the marriage and relationship that He has with His bride (us). He shows us by example how to govern, how to guide, and most important of all, how to love. If we take all that He shows us and bring it into our marriage, our family, our church, our jobs, and our communities, then we will be the men God wants us to be.

It used to be said, "Behind every good man, there is a good woman." Not so, in most cases today. Women are leading us men, dragging us along and we have let it happen. We have allowed the ERA and other women's organizations to change the way we think. Not only have our wives come to agree with them, but many of us Christian men are agreeing with them as well. Fifty-fifty, equal-equal. It won't work! We are not equal. We are not the same. We were not created the same. We have different functions. We have different roles. God's plan for us doesn't need to be adjusted by the world. It is perfect and works perfectly if we are willing to walk in it, in obedience to His Word.

# 5

# The Heart

*But there was a certain man called Simon, who previously practiced sorcery in the city and astonished the people of Samaria, claiming that he was someone great, [10] to whom they all gave heed, from the least to the greatest, saying, "This man is the great power of God." [11] And they heeded him because he had astonished them with his sorceries for a long time. [12] But when they believed Philip as he preached the things concerning the kingdom of God and the name of Jesus Christ, both men and women were baptized. [13] **Then Simon himself also believed; and when he was baptized** he continued with Philip, and was amazed, seeing the miracles and signs which were done. [14] Now when the apostles who were at Jerusalem heard that Samaria had received the word of God, they sent Peter and John to them, [15] who, when they had come down, prayed for them that they might receive the Holy Spirit. [16] For as yet He had fallen upon none of them. They had only been baptized in the name of the Lord Jesus. [17] Then they laid hands on them, and they received the Holy Spirit. [18] And when Simon saw that through the laying on of the apostles' hands the Holy Spirit was given, he offered them money, [19] saying, "Give me this power also, that anyone on whom I lay* *hands may receive the Holy Spirit." [20] But Peter said to him, "Your money perish with you, because you thought that the gift of God could be purchased with money! [21] You have neither part nor portion in this matter, **for your heart is not right in the sight of God.** [22] Repent therefore of this your wickedness, and pray God if perhaps the thought of your heart may be forgiven you. [23] For I see that you are poisoned by bitterness and **bound by iniquity**.*

*(Acts 8:9-23)*

Simon was a baptized believer and most likely a member of Philip's fellowship. He was amazed at all the signs and wonders which were done. (vs.13) He wanted to be part of that. He saw the power come through Peter and John when they laid hands on the people and prayed. He thought " the more money I put into this fellowship, the more I will be recognized as a leader, and then I will be given this same power." (vs.19) Peter answered him in verse twenty-one, "You have neither part nor portion in this matter, <u>**for your heart is not right in the sight of God.**</u>" What a blow that must have been for this baptized believer: "Your heart is not right in the sight of God." I can almost hear Simon, "But I said all the words you told me to say, repeated the words you prayed with me. I went down to the lake, and you were there. You saw it: I went under for Jesus." **But, your heart is not right in the sight of God.**

> *'These people draw near to Me with their mouth, And honor Me with their lips, But their heart is far from Me.*
>
> *(Matthew 15:8)*

There are over 800 scriptures in the Bible pertaining to the heart. Most of them deal with knowing our hearts, looking into our hearts, or changing our hearts.

> *And He said to them, "You are those who justify yourselves before men, but God knows your hearts. For what is highly esteemed among men is an abomination in the sight of God.*
>
> *(Luke 16:15)*

What a scary thought ! He knows our hearts. If our hearts are not pure before Him, then we will not be pleasing in His sight.

> *Draw near to God and He will draw near to you. Cleanse your hands, you sinners; and purify your hearts, you double-minded.*
>
> *(James 4:8)*

"To Purify" means "to remove whatever renders unclean and unfit for sacred service." (Webster's 1828)

*O Jerusalem, wash your heart from wickedness,*
*That you may be saved. How long shall your evil*
*thoughts lodge within you?*

*(Jeremiah 4:14)*

It is so important that we constantly and consistently search our hearts and remove the plagued stones that are keeping us from a closer walk with the Lord.

There is a story in Leviticies 14:33-42 about the leprous plagued stones in a certain man's house. The priest has to go in and remove the stones and cast them into an unclean place outside the city. Then the house is to be scraped and cleaned. We have plagued stones in our hearts that must be removed. Oftentimes our hearts are the home for bitterness, resentment, unforgiveness, anger, hatred, rebellion, greed, lust, deceit, selfishness, arrogance, and pride.

Most of us men do not want to look into our own hearts. We can tell everyone else what to do, but search our own hearts? That's a no-no!

*Every way of a man is right in his own eyes,* ***But***
***the LORD weighs the hearts.***

*(Proverbs 21:2)*

*"The heart is deceitful above all things, And desperately wicked; Who can know it? [10]* ***I, the***
***LORD, search the heart, I test the mind"***

*(Jeremiah 17:9-10)*

*But the LORD said to Samuel, "Do not look at his appearance or at the height of his stature, because I have refused him. **For the Lord does not see as man sees; for man looks at the outward appearance, but the LORD looks at the heart."***

*(1 Samuel 16:7)*

*"As for you, my son Solomon, know the God of your father, and serve Him with a loyal heart and with a willing mind; **for the LORD searches all hearts and understands all the intent of the thoughts**. If you seek Him, He will be found by you; but if you forsake Him, He will cast you off forever."*

*(1Chronicles 28:9)*

**Create in me a clean heart, O God, And renew a steadfast spirit within me.**

*(Psalms 51:10*

This verse should be our constant prayer. I remember when I was challenged by a preacher to pray this verse everyday, to start my day by praying, "Create in me a clean heart, O Lord." I decided to take his advice, and what the Lord showed me changed my life. I thought that I was okay, that praying that verse wouldn't be much of a challenge. I was wrong. The Lord started waking me up in the middle of the night. It was then that He revealed to me that most of the problems that were happening with our family were my fault. I was taken aback.

**My** fault!? Why, Lord I read Your Word every day! I go to church every week! I'm an elder in my church! I am president of a businessmen's fellowship chapter! People come to me when they have problems! And You are saying that I am responsible for most of these problems! I've never been a person who cries. My father taught me that real men don't cry. But, after the Lord got ahold of my heart, I cried for six months. Sometimes for no reason that I knew I would be just having a conversation with someone and I would start crying. God was changing my heart. It is a lie of the enemy that men don't cry. Real men should be able to show their emotions. I now cry at super market openings.

*Then I will sprinkle clean water on you, and you shall be clean; I will cleanse you from all your filthiness and from all your idols. [26] I will give you a new heart and put a new spirit within you; I will take the heart of stone out of your flesh and give you a heart of flesh. [27] I will put My Spirit within you and cause you to walk in My statutes, and you will keep My judgments and do them.*
*(Ezekiel 36:25-27)*

The heart referred to in the scriptures is not the physical heart that pumps our blood. It is the very center of our being.

Webster's 1828 dictionary says: "The heart is the inner part of anything, the middle part or interior, the chief part, the vital part, the seat of the affections and passions as love, joy.

We see that a man's heart can be hardened:

*Therefore, as the Holy Spirit says: "Today, if you will hear His voice, [8] Do not harden your hearts as in the rebellion, In the day of trial in the wilderness, [9] Where your fathers tested Me, tried Me, And saw My works forty years.[10] Therefore I was angry with that generation, And said, 'They always go astray in their heart, And they have not known My ways.' [11] So I swore in My wrath, 'They shall not enter My rest.' "[12] Beware, brethren, lest there be in any of you an evil heart of unbelief in departing from the living God;*

*(Hebrews 3:7-12)*

We are to love with our hearts:

*And to love Him with all the heart, with all the understanding, with all the soul, and with all the strength, and to love one's neighbor as oneself, is more than all the whole burnt offerings and sacrifices."*

*(Mark 12:33)*

We can doubt with our hearts:

*For assuredly, I say to you, whoever says to this mountain, 'Be removed and be cast into the sea,' and does not doubt in his heart, but believes that those things he says will be done, he will have whatever he says.*

*(Mark 11:23)*

45

We can serve with our hearts:

*'And it shall be that if you earnestly obey My com-
mandments which I command you today, to love the
LORD your God and serve Him with all your heart
and with all your soul,*

*(Deuteronomy 11:13)*

Our hearts can rejoice; they can deceive; they
can be sick; they can be anxious; they can be
afraid; and the list goes on and on. Our hearts are
the very center of our beings. It is where we live.

What does asking God to search our hearts and
being willing to examine our own hearts and identify the plagued stones have to do with our living
out our roles as men, husbands, and fathers? **Just
everything!** We cannot be what God wants us to
be until we are willing to look into our own hearts
and see ourselves as we are. We must clean out the
old things of the world, the old thinking, the old
ways, and replace them with God's way, God's
thinking, and Godly things.

If we want all of what God has for us, we must
give Him all we have.

## Each must give his whole heart to Him:

## In Love:

*You shall love the LORD your God with all your
heart, with all your soul, and with all your strength*

*(Deuteronomy 6:5)*

## In Obedience:

*Blessed are those who keep His testimonies, Who seek Him with the whole heart!*

*(Psalms 119:2)*

## In Trust:

*Trust in the LORD with all your heart, And lean not on your own understanding;*

*(Proverbs 3:5)*

## In Prayer:

*And you will seek Me and find Me, when you search for Me with all your heart.*

*(Jeremiah 29:13)*

## In Repentance:

*"Now, therefore," says the LORD, "Turn to Me with all your heart, With fasting, with weeping, and with mourning." [13] So rend your heart, and not your garments; Return to the LORD your God, For He is gracious and merciful, Slow to anger, and of great kindness; And He relents from doing harm.*

*(Joel 2:12-13)*

Remember, "to rend" means "to tear apart," sometimes viciously. It is time for us men to yield our hearts to the Lord and to allow Him to do the necessary tearing to remove those plagued stones.

# 6

## Headship

*Pattern yourselves after me (follow my example), as I imitate and follow Christ (the Messiah). I appreciate and commend you because you always remember me in everything and keep firm possession of the traditions (the substance of my instructions), just as I have (verbally) passed them on to you. But I want you to know and realize that Christ is the Head of every man, the head of a woman is her husband and the Head of Christ is God.*

*(1 Corinthians 11:1-3 AMP.)*

Webster's 1828 dictionary says, "The head, is to lead, to direct, to act as leader, authority, chief place, a chief, a principal person, a leader, one who has the first rank or place, and to whom others are subordinate."

Do you think that is what the Holy Spirit meant when He inspired Paul to impress on us that Christ is the Head of the man? That Christ is the One who leads, directs, and *is* the authority? That Christ is the One who takes chief place, has first rank or place? That Christ is the One to whom we are subordinate (lesser, dependent, subservient)?

If we can say "Yes" to this, how about the next line?; "The head of a woman is her husband."

48

He is the one who leads, directs, and *is* the authority. He is the one who takes chief place, has first rank or place. He is the one to whom the family is subordinate (lesser, dependent, subservient).

We have an enormous responsibility as the heads of our wives and our families. We men will have to give an account some day of how we guided those entrusted to us.

*So then each of us shall give account of himself to God.*
*(Romans 14:12)*

Do you think that the wives of today or the children of today are turning to their heads? In most cases, the wives are not turning to their heads because the men are not <u>turning to theirs</u>. We need to spend time with Him every day. We have to learn to hear His voice and get to know Him as a person. Jesus said in John 8:19 "You know neither Me, nor my Father..." (What one is saying when he says "You don't know me, is, "The me that you <u>think</u> I am is not the me that I am). When we men really get to know Him then we can lead and direct our wives and families according to His Word.

It is a chain of command:

## GOD
## CHRIST
## MAN
## WOMAN

I've heard some men say, "Jesus doesn't talk to me." If that is the case, then we have to ask:

1. Am I spending enough time with Him?

2. Am I listening or just talking?

I can guarantee you, that if you will take time every day to be by yourself before God, empty out your mind and pray and listen, you *will* hear from God. You *will* hear His voice. I can guarantee it because the Word says it.

> *And you will seek Me and find Me, when you search for Me with all your heart.*
>
> *(Jeremiah 29:13)*

He wants to give us direction. He wants to deal with the one whom He created to be the head of the family. I often think about Mary and Joseph. Mary, blessed among all women, gave birth to the Savior of the world. But when it was time for them to leave Bethlehem and flee to Egypt, whom did God instruct? The head of the family, Joseph.

Can you imagine a woman of today submitting to an uncomfortable ride like that without a word of protest? Today's woman would be sure that her husband had missed God's voice. But, maybe Mary trusted him and felt secure with his decision because she knew he was a man who sought God for direction. Maybe he was a man who was easy to submit to because she knew he was in touch with God.

If we were like Joseph, seeking the Lord and being obedient to His will, our wives might be more willing to obey us. God cannot be pleased when all those distraught anxious women come to Him for help with issues that their husbands, the heads, should be taking care of.

It was prophesied in Isaiah 3:12 —

*As for My people, children are their oppressors, And women rule over them, O My people! Those who lead you to err, And destroy the way of your paths."*

God did not design the woman to be the head of the man. Women are not happy when they are in control. When the roles are reversed they become contentious.

*A continual dripping on a very rainy day And a contentious woman are alike; [16] Whoever restrains her restrains the wind, And grasps oil with his right hand.*
*(Proverbs 27:15-16)*

A contentious woman is one who is given to angry debate, quarrelsome. Her anger is often caused by a husband who is not taking authority and does not have a Godly attitude. He is a **Faker**. His Christianity is apparent on Sunday mornings and Wednesday nights at bible study. When it comes to the home, it is a different story. This isn't good enough for our wives. This isn't good enough for God.

We are to be imitators of Jesus, all the time.

*Therefore be imitators of God as dear children.*
*(Ephesians 5:1)*

Jesus came with a three-fold ministry.

## Priest — Prophet — King

*Priest — As He also says in another place:"You are a priest forever according to the order of Melchizedek",*

*(Hebrews 5:6)*

The Priest is the one who is in charge of spiritual matters. We are called to be the Priest. We are the ones who should be leading our families in prayer, reading of the scripture, making sure that the truths of God are taught to our children. God has called us to be the spiritual leaders in our homes. Why do we see so many married women in prayer lines? Because their husbands are not doing their jobs as the Priest of their homes. The husbands are not praying with their wives or ministering God's Word to them when they have needs.

*Prophet — I will raise up for them a Prophet like you from among their brethren, and will put My words in His mouth, and He shall speak to them all that I command Him.*

*(Deuteronomy 18:18)*

The Prophet is the one who is instructed by God. Oh! How beautiful our lives would be if we husbands were consistently praying, seeking the Lord, and getting His instructions for our families and our homes. We **must** set time aside every day to just <u>be</u> before Him. Big corporations have staff meetings every day before the days work begins. This is done so that each department can hear from its head. Necessary changes can be made. New ideas and new direction can be implemented where needed. We need to seek guidance from our Head. We need to hear from Him.

*King — took branches of palm trees and went out to meet Him, and cried out:"Hosanna! 'Blessed is He who comes in the name of the LORD!' The King of Israel!"*

*(John 12:13)*

The **King** came not to be waited on but to serve.

*just as the Son of Man did not come to be served, but to serve, and to give His life a ransom for many."*

*(Matthew 20:28)*

Most of us think of a king as one who shouts orders and makes demands on everyone around him, one whose every need is met by those under him, similar to a drill sergeant. "Hail to the King!" We can go along with this idea, but when it comes to a king being a servant, that's a different story. I believe that a Christian woman whose husband is imitating Jesus and following His example, would have no problem being a helpmate and submitting to him as unto the Lord. We can depend on Jesus. He is always there when we need Him. He will never put us off when we need someone to talk to or someone to dump our problems on. He is never loud or overbearing. He is never demanding. He is always loving, caring, and interested in all our needs no matter how trivial they are. When we are in His presence, we feel safe and secure. He is gentle, but we know He is the one who is in charge. He is not a dictator, but He is the Head. He is our example of how to live out our kingship. Is this the way our wives see us?

We men are easily led and often misguided by our wives. This happened to me recently. My wife and I had made plans to go to a week-end convention. We both were looking forward to it for a long time. Then some things came up that made me question whether or not we should go, one of them being that my car broke down. I would have to rent a car and felt that I didn't need that extra expense at the time. I expressed that to Gene a couple of times and asked her how she would feel about canceling. She was disappointed that I was considering changing the plans, and she said, "Oh!, we shouldn't worry about money. God will supply all our needs" (note the scripture). We talked about it a little more, and I gave in, rented a car and we went. Well, to make a long story short, we were both uncomfortable all week-end and felt we shouldn't have been there. Gene felt bad and knew she had influenced my decision and was blaming herself. But it wasn't her fault; it was mine. If she had agreed to a change of plans right away, I would have changed them. But because she didn't, I gave in. I made two mistakes:

1. I didn't pray about it. I should have gone off by myself and sought the Lord for his direction and then prayed with her. I'm sure then we both would have found the mind of the Lord about it.
2. Because I listened to my wife and wanted to please her, I ignored the check in my spirit and what God was trying to say to me, and I just wimped out.

Another thing about it. We reaped what we sowed! We got out of God's perfect will (even though we were praising Him all week-end), missed out on some special opportunities, and it took us some time to get back on track. This is why moment-by-moment communication with Him is so important!

Many times in the scripture we see that the man failed God because of the woman.

- Adam failed God because he listened to his wife. (Genesis 3:17)
- Abraham, instead of believing God, listened to his wife, went into Hagar, and Ishmael was born. We are still living with the results of that today. (Genesis 16:2-3)
- Moses was almost killed by God. God told him to circumcise his son, but he wouldn't do it because his wife opposed it. (Exodus 4:24-25. Amplified)
- David, the greatest of all the Kings of Israel, committed adultery with Bathsheba, Uriah's wife and had him killed. (2 Samuel 11: 1-27)
- Samson was tempted, deceived, and destroyed by a woman. (Judges 16)
- Solomon, a man of wisdom and foolishness, had seven hundred wives and three hundred concubines. (1 Kings 11:1-4)

Am I saying that our wives lead us astray all the time? NO, NO, NO, a thousand times NO. My greatest gift is the helpmate God has given me. But women have a great deal of power over a man. They have that which man needs to be fulfilled.

Man is incomplete without woman. When God created man, he was complete, but when He created the woman, He took a part of the man, and man needs that part back to be complete. (Gen. 2:21-23)

Men desire to please their wives and keep them contented because it makes for a happier house and a pleasant place to come home to.

*Better to dwell in a corner of a housetop, Than in a house shared with a contentious woman.*

*(Proverbs 21:9)*

But, we try to please them in the wrong way. We give in to them and give our headship over to them. I see this happening more and more. If you go to purchase something with your wife, notice how the sales person will direct the sales pitch to her. Go to a restaurant; stand before the hostess and watch how in most cases she will ask the woman, "How many, and where would you like to sit?" When it is time to pay the bill, many times it is the woman who will take the bill, check it over, take the money out of her purse and bring it to the cashier. When children need permission to do something or need money, they go to their mothers rather than their fathers. Now you may be thinking that these observations are petty, but they are not. They are examples of how men are releasing their headship to women.

It's all very subtle. It starts with the little things, and before you know it, the man is nothing more than a paycheck. Some of you, I am sure, feel just like that.

This has to change! Men have to come back to their God-given position to be the heads of their homes. It's not going to be easy. We will have to come at it in a Christ-like manner, gently and lovingly. We will have to be determined to take God's principles and teachings, study them, and put them into practice. A man who has to tell his wife, his children, his friends, and neighbors that he is the boss, usually isn't. That is not the way Jesus did it. Jesus loved; Jesus taught; Jesus encouraged; Jesus led. And they all knew by His actions that He had authority.

> *But I want you to know that the head of every man is Christ, the head of woman is man, and the head of Christ is God.*
>
> *(1 Corinthians 11:3)*

# 7

# Parenting

Understanding God's plan of authority in the home is crucial to the success of child rearing. The man is the head.

*For the husband is head of the wife, as also Christ is head of the church; and He is the Savior of the body. [24] Therefore, just as the church is subject to Christ, so let the wives be to their own husbands in everything.*

*(Ephesians 5:23-24)*

*The living, the living man, he shall praise You, As I do this day; The father shall make known Your truth to the children.*

*(Isaiah 38:19)*

We are the head and we are to make known the truths to our children. We are to teach, train and discipline them.

## 1. To Teach:

*"And these words which I command you today shall be in your heart. [7] You shall teach them diligently to your children, and shall talk of them when you sit in your house, when you walk by the way, when you lie down, and when you rise up.*

*(Deuteronomy 6:6-7)*

*"Only take heed to yourself, and diligently keep yourself, lest you forget the things your eyes have seen, and lest they depart from your heart all the days of your life. And teach them to your children and your grandchildren ...*

*(Deuteronomy 4:9)*

*For He established a testimony in Jacob, And appointed a law in Israel, Which He commanded our fathers, That they should make them known to their children.*

*(Psalm 78:5)*

This is pretty clear. It is the father's responsibility to make known the truth of God to the children. This cannot be done just by the children attending Children's Church or Sunday School or even a Christian school. There should be time set aside every day to teach our children about God and His ways, and it is the father's responsibility to see that this is done. Teaching is necessary. Sitting down and reading God's Word together is important and should be done on a regular basis. But, also they see the examples in our homes: The way a husband treats his wife, the way a father talks to his children, the way a husband and wife talk about their neighbors and friends, what is watched on television, what kind of magazines are around the house. All these things have a great influence on our children.

## 2. **To Train:**

*Train up a child in the way he should go, And when he is old he will not depart from it.*

*(Proverbs 22:6)*

*And you, fathers, do not provoke your children to wrath, but bring them up in the training and admonition of the Lord.*

*(Ephesians 6:4)*

Unfortunately, many children are left by themselves a good part of the day. And it is the television that is training them. The television can be a curse in our homes. It steals time. It kills initiative. It destroys relationships. It should be used sparingly and with careful supervision.

*The thief does not come except to steal, and to kill, and to destroy. I have come that they may have life, and that they may have it more abundantly.*

*(John 10:10)*

I read somewhere that the average American father gives thirty-five seconds of **undivided** attention to his child per day.

*The rod and rebuke give wisdom, But a child left to himself brings shame to his mother.*

*(Proverbs 29:15)*

Children are an extension of a husband and a wife's relationship. They are given to us by God.

61

*And he lifted his eyes and saw the women and children, and said, "Who are these with you?" So he said, "The children whom God has graciously given your servant."*

*(Genesis 33:5)*

*And Joseph said to his father "They are my sons, whom God has given me in this place." And he said, "Please bring them to me, and I will bless them."*

*(Genesis 48:9)*

*Here am I and the children whom the LORD has given me!*

*(Isaiah 8:18)*

We don't *own* our children. We didn't create them. We didn't purchase them. They are a gift from God. This is important to understand. It will save a lot of heartaches in later years, when the scripture is fulfilled, and they leave their father and mother. (Genesis 2:24)

### 3. To Discipline:

*He who spares his rod hates his son, But he who loves him disciplines him promptly.*

*(Proverbs 13:24)*

*Chasten your son while there is hope, And do not set your heart on his destruction.*

*(Proverbs 19:18)*

Webster's 1828 Dictionary says, "to chasten" is "to correct by punishment, to inflict pain."

*Do not withhold correction from a child, For if you beat him with a rod, he will not die. [14] You shall beat him with a rod, And deliver his soul from hell.*
*(Proverbs 23:13-14)*

*Foolishness is bound up in the heart of a child; The rod of correction will drive it far from him.*
*(Proverbs 22:15)*

The word for "Rod" in the Hebrew language is "shay-bet". It literally means "a stick for punishing."

Many books have been written on how to discipline and to raise Godly children. The very best one is the Bible. It surpasses all other books because it is God's way, and His way never fails.

*So shall My word be that goes forth from My mouth;It shall not return to Me void, But it shall accomplish what I please, And it shall prosper in the thing for which I sent it.*
*(Isaiah 55:11)*

When disciplining children, it is very important to be firm, consistent, and loving.

### A.) Be Firm:

Speak with authority. Do not yell or scream. Speaking with authority means saying what you mean and meaning what you say.

*But let your communication be, Yea, yea; Nay, nay:*
*for whatsoever is more than these cometh of evil.*

*(Matthew 5:37 KJV)*

As an authority figure, set a good example so that your children will develop a healthy attitude towards authority. Children watch their parents. Do you obey the speed limit, respect stop signs and red lights? What do your children hear you say about the policeman directing the traffic, or about the leaders of our country, or about their teachers, or about the leaders of our churches, or about anyone who is in authority over you?

Don't be wishy-washy. Some psychiatrists and psychologists will tell us to be buddies with our children and to meet them at their level. It sounds like good advice, but it can be deceiving. It can blur the fact that they are the children and we are the fathers. We don't need our children communicating with us as if they were our friends, as equals. This does not line up with the Word of God. The patriachs of the Old Testament expected and received the respect and honor that was due them right up to their deaths. Some parents actually fear that they will lose their children's love if they are firm. No! They will love you more and be more secure in your love if they know their limits.

**B.) Be Consistent:**

If you say you are going to punish a child ... Do it. If you are not going to do it — **Don't say it.** Sometimes we say the stupidest things to our children. Do you want a spanking? "Uh! Sure Dad! I would love one. I've been waiting all day for you to ask me!" Screaming and yelling at children and threatening them with a spanking if they don't stop misbehaving is a waste of time and words. Children know how far they can go before they have to stop. They have been taught that by the tone of their parent's voices. Have the rod in your house in a visible, place and when there is a need for discipline, get it and use it.

Why? Because God's Word says so.

How? Calmly (**Never** discipline when you are angry).

Where? A safe area of the anatomy where it can do no harm.

After you have disciplined a child and he has stopped crying, go to him, give him a hug and explain to him that his behavior earned him that punishment. Ask him if he is sorry, and when he is, offer him forgiveness and pray together.

Be sure that your children know beforehand what their limits are, what you expect of them, and what they can expect to be punished for. Be careful not to major in minors. I believe the rod is God's way to train young children, but it is not to be used when a child has made natural mistakes i.e., spilling the milk etc. It is not to be used to try to make them into clones of ourselves. It is for overt rebellion. If child discipline is a problem in your home, you and your wife need to study together, and you as the head will need to set the guidelines.

You will find that after just a few days of this kind of discipline, the rod will collect dust.

Don't give out punishments that are going to cause inconvenience to the rest of the family. Sometimes we put restrictions on our children that restrict the whole family, or we put on restrictions that are unreasonable, that we cannot carry through, and we have to back down. That is not consistent. Think before you give out punishments.

When you are at home, take charge of the discipline. When you are not, leave instructions for your wife to carry out. The father is the one to set the rules for the family. Children know who should be in charge. They will accept the discipline of their father if it is given in the proper way.

### C.) Be Loving:

The strongest force in the world is love. This is without a doubt the most important part of disciplining children.

Gene and I have been blessed with four of the greatest kids in the world. I was a very strong disciplinarian, and they were very well-behaved youngsters. Wherever we were, all it took was one look from Dad, and they got the message. I was using biblical principles before I even knew what biblical principles were, with one exception. I left out the most important principle of all. I left out love. My children obeyed me because they feared me. I was a hard taskmaster. My love was conditional. Do things right and you were loved. Do things wrong and the love was withdrawn. Jesus loves us no matter what we do. He doesn't approve of our rebellious behavior, but He still loves us. I loved my children deep in my heart, but I couldn't show it on the surface unless they were meeting my strict demands. The love was not unconditional.

The Bible says if we love our children, we will discipline them promptly. Don't worry about your child's love for you. If you teach a child in love, if you train a child in love, if you discipline a child in love, that child will grow up, taught, trained, and disciplined and they will love you for it.

Now, for those whose children are beyond parents' authority, for those who feel that they have failed, the good news is that God promises restoration.

*"So I will restore to you the years that the swarming locust has eaten, The crawling locust, The consuming locust, And the chewing locust, My great army which I sent among you.*

*(Joel 2:25)*

Maybe if we knew then, what we know now, things would have been different. But we didn't know. It is so important to turn them over to God. Don't you try to change them. (If I can just get them to read this, that will do it, or if I can just get them to go hear this preacher, that will do it). If this describes you, then you obviously have not turned them over to God. Don't preach to them. Be an example. Pray for them. Admit your mistakes to them. Be firm in what you believe. Be consistent in your walk. But most of all, be loving. Love them through their trials. Also, remember that you are the head of the home. You are the authority, and although they have reached adulthood, if they are still living at home, they are to respect and follow the rules you have set.

We teach, train, and discipline our children by instructing them. We also teach, train, and discipline by our example, by how we act ourselves. How we operate in our daily lives has a great influence on the images our children will take into adulthood:

The image of what a man should be.

The image of what a father should be.

The image of what a husband should be.
The image of what the head of the family should be.

*If your sons will keep My covenant And My testimony which I shall teach them, Their sons also shall sit upon your throne forevermore."*

*(Psalm 132:12)*

# 8

# Rebellion

Men, we know that we are not fulfilling our roles as the heads of our homes. It's much easier to sit ourselves down in front of the television and to let the women do it. Someone once asked Katherine Kulman why she did what she did, and her reply was "Because the men will not do it." The men (most men) are not willing to pay the price of denying self and dying daily.

It is not just in the home that we see women in places of authority. We now have policepeople, firepeople, women in combat in the military, and women in government in high ranking positions leading the men.

> As for My people, children are their oppressors, And women rule over them. O My people! Those who lead you cause you to err, And destroy the way of your paths.
>
> *(Isaiah 3:12)*

"As for my people, children are their oppressors" (An oppressor is one who imposes unjust burdens on others), "and women rule over them." It is not unusual for us to see strong, healthy men staying at home, taking care of the children, doing the housekeeping while the women are out working, providing for the family. It's all backwards. Man has relinquished his role as the head of the home and women are in positions that God did not plan for them.

We are rebelling against God's authority and against His Word.

*"Woe to the rebellious children," says the LORD, "Who take counsel, but not of Me, And who devise plans, but not of My Spirit, That they may add sin to sin;*

*(Isaiah 30:1)*

What is rebellion? Webster's 1828 Dictionary says that "rebellion is open resistance to lawful authority."

What does the Bible say that it is.

*For rebellion is as the sin of witchcraft, And stubbornness is as iniquity and idolatry.* **Because you have rejected the word of the LORD,** *He also has rejected you from being king.*

*(1 Samuel 15:23)*

"Rebellion is as the sin of witchcraft." Witchcraft is intercourse with the devil. (Webster's 1828)

These words in 1 Samuel 15:23 were spoken to King Saul to whom God had spoken and commanded to go and utterly destroy the Amalekites.

Saul felt he had obeyed God because he destroyed the Amalekites, but he let the people take plunder, sheep, and oxen to sacrifice to the Lord. Look at 1 Samuel 15:22:

*So Samuel said: "Has the LORD as great delight in burnt offerings and sacrifices, As in obeying the voice of the LORD? Behold, to obey is better than sacrifice, ...*

Saul thought he was doing a good thing, but he was not obeying God and because of that God rejected him as king. So many times in the scripture we see God's anger and wrath because of rebellion.

Hananiah the prophet died because he taught rebellion against the Lord.

*Therefore thus says the LORD: 'Behold, I will cast you from the face of the earth. This year you shall die, because you have taught rebellion against the LORD.' [17] So Hananiah the prophet died the same year in the seventh month.*

*(Jeremiah 28:16-17)*

Descendants would not be blessed.

*... therefore thus says the LORD: Behold, I will punish Shemaiah the Nehelamite and his family: he shall not have anyone to dwell among this people, nor shall he see the good that I will do for My people, says the LORD, because he has taught rebellion against the LORD.*

*(Jeremiah 29:32)*

## Babies and pregnant women were brutalized.

*Samaria is held guilty, For she has rebelled against her God. They shall fall by the sword, Their infants shall be dashed in pieces, And their women with child ripped open.*

*(Hosea 13:16)*

## Entire nations were punished.

*"Thus says the whole congregation of the LORD: 'What treachery is this that you have committed against the God of Israel, to turn away this day from following the LORD, in that you have built for yourselves an altar, that you might rebel this day against the LORD? [17] Is the iniquity of Peor not enough for us, from which we are not cleansed until this day, although there was a plague in the congregation of the LORD, [18] but that you must turn away this day from following the LORD? And it shall be, if you rebel today against the LORD, that tomorrow He will be angry with the whole congregation of Israel. [19] Nevertheless, if the land of your possession is unclean, then cross over to the land of the possession of the LORD, where the LORD'S tabernacle stands, and take possession among us; but do not rebel against the LORD, nor rebel against us, by building yourselves an altar besides the altar of the LORD our God. [20] Did not Achan the son of Zerah commit a trespass in the accursed thing, and wrath fell on all the congregation of Israel? And that man did not perish alone in his iniquity.'*

*(Joshua 22:16-20)*

Rebellion is a serious condition in the eyes of God. We cannot afford to be rebellious. Consider the Israelites coming out of Egypt. Forty years it took for an eleven day journey. They kept having to take another turn around the mountain because of their rebellion. We cannot afford to rebel against God and what he has planned and designed for us. Man has been rebelling against God from the beginning. God in His pursuit of righteous men who will do what is in the mind and heart of God has been held back over and over because of rebellious hearts. This rebellious spirit is most evident in our homes. This is where it first manifests itself. God has given us a wonderful handbook with which to direct our lives: His Word. It is time for us to obey it.

# 9

# Bitterness

*Husbands, love your wives and do not be bitter toward them.*

*(Colossians 3:19)*

There are many plagued stones in our hearts that we must dig up, and cast out of our lives, in order to walk in freedom. One that seems to be deeply rooted in us is bitterness. It is like a cancer. It forces us out of relationship with God. It destroys our manhood and ruins our marriages.

"Bitter" means: "sharp, cruel, severe, sarcastic, hurtful, painful to the mind." (Webster's 1828)

The Bible says the key to a successful marriage is to love our wives as Jesus loved the church.

*Wives, submit to your own husbands, as to the Lord. [23] For the husband is head of the wife, as also Christ is head of the church; and He is the Savior of the body. [24] Therefore, just as the church is subject to Christ, so let the wives be to their own husbands in everything. [25] Husbands, love your wives, just as Christ also loved the church and gave Himself for her, [26] that He might sanctify and cleanse her with the washing of water by the word, [27] that He might present her to Himself a glorious church, not having spot or*

*wrinkle or any such thing, but that she should be holy and without blemish. [28] So husbands ought to love their own wives as their own bodies; he who loves his wife loves himself. [29] For no one ever hated his own flesh, but nourishes and cherishes it, just as the Lord does the church. [30] For we are members of His body, of His flesh and of His bones.*
*(Ephesians 5:22-30)*

I like the way verses 25-30 read in the Living Bible " ... and you husbands, show the same kind of love to your wives as Christ showed to the church when He died for her, washed by baptism and God's Word; so that He could give her to Himself as a glorious church without a single spot or wrinkle or any other blemish, being holy and without a single fault." This is how husbands should treat their wives, loving them as part of themselves. For since a man and his wife are now one, a man is really doing himself a favor and loving himself when he loves his wife. No one hates his own body but lovingly cares for it, just as Christ cares for His body the church, of which we are a part.

We are to love our own wives just as Jesus loves His church. When Jesus came to earth He was a lowly, humble, servant.

*... just as the Son of Man did not come to be served, but to serve, and to give His life a ransom for many.*
*(Matthew 20:28)*

76

Jesus was not an "I" man. He was not worried about His ego or pride.

*Servants, be submissive to your masters with all fear, not only to the good and gentle, but also to the harsh. [19] For this is commendable, if because of conscience toward God one endures grief, suffering wrongfully. [20] For what credit is it if, when you are beaten for your faults, you take it patiently? But when you do good and suffer, if you take it patiently, this is commendable before God. [21] For to this you were called, because Christ also suffered for us, leaving us an example, that you should follow His steps:[22] "Who committed no sin, Nor was deceit found in His mouth"; [23] who, when He was reviled, did not revile in return; when He suffered, He did not threaten, but committed Himself to Him who judges righteously;*

*(1 Peter 2:18-23)*

In looking at the above verses we see that Peter is talking about the crucifixion of Jesus. He talks about doing good and suffering for it, and if we take it patiently, that pleases God. He says that we were called to this because Christ suffered for us leaving us an example, that we should follow in His steps. It goes on to say how He committed no sin, that no guile was found in His mouth and when He was reviled, He did not revile in return. Then in chapter 3, verse 1 it says: "Likewise, you wives" and again in verse 7, "likewise you husbands." What is being said here is that in order for a wife to submit to her husband, it may take some suffering on her part. And in order for a husband to dwell with his wife with understanding, giving honor, it might take some suffering on his part.

This suffering is not a physical suffering. It's a hurt to our pride and our ego. It is death to self and a putting down of our flesh. It is painful.

Webster's 1828 says: "Egotism is the practice of too frequently using the word 'I', speaking or writing much of one's self, self praise, self commendation, the act or practice of magnifying one's self or making one's self of importance."

Our ego is the area that is ever too ready to birth the seeds of bitterness. Seeds of bitterness can take root and we don't even know they are there. They become plagued stones in our hearts and they must be removed.

### How do we get rid of them?

1. Ask God to show us the areas of bitterness.
2. Recognize that they are a problem to us.
3. Talk it over with our wives.
4. Pray about it together.
5. Ask forgiveness for allowing them in.
6. Give them to God.
7. Thank Him for His deliverance and forgiveness.

These seeds of bitterness can get implanted in us, very easily by something that was said or done.

For example, here are some secret thoughts men might have which could turn into plagued stones of bitterness:

She forced me into marriage.

She put financial burdens on me.

She spent the money I wanted to save or invest or use for a vacation.

She kept me from accepting a job I thought would be right.

She kept me from completing my education.

She mocked me sexually.

She resisted me sexually.

She was unfaithful to me.

She tried to mother me.

She nags and embarrasses me in front of others.

She refuses to go with me to meetings or social events.

She dislikes my mother whom I love.

She shared our personal problems with her mother, and her girl friends, and that makes me feel foolish.

She insists on going out with friends I don't approve of.

She constantly reminds me of my mistakes and failures.

She prevented me from buying property.

She influenced me to move where I did not want to live.

She agreed to move but never adapted to it, and had a bad attitude.

She pressured me into allowing our children to do things I was against.

She pressured me to put more restrictions on our children than I thought they should have.

She refused to have children.

She had an abortion, against my wishes.

She influenced me to attend a church, I didn't want to be at.

She has a spiritually superior attitude towards me.

She refuses to go places with me, or take a vacation with me, because she says she would be bored.

She is constantly telling me what to do and no matter what I do, she still is not pleased.

Any of these thoughts and many others, can plant a seed of bitterness in our hearts which can grow into a plagued stone causing a huge stumbling block, not only in our marriage but in our relationship with God. Bitterness keeps us concentrated on the other person's faults, and therefore our minds are not centered on our Lord and Savior Jesus Christ.

We must be willing to be honest with ourselves and with God. We may have adjusted to some of these hurts, but the bitterness is still there, just covered up or buried. Hurts that are covered up and hidden live in darkness. Satan reigns in darkness. Bring the hurts and bitterness to the light. **Jesus reigns in light.**

# 10

# The Tongue

*And the tongue is a fire, a world of iniquity. The
tongue is so set among our members that it defiles
the whole body, and sets on fire the course of
nature; and it is set on fire by hell. [7] For every
kind of beast and bird, of reptile and creature of the
sea, is tamed and has been tamed by mankind. [8]
But no man can tame the tongue. It is an unruly
evil, full of deadly poison. [9] With it we bless our
God and Father, and with it we curse men, who
have been made in the similitude of God. [10] Out
of the same mouth proceed blessing and cursing.
My brethren, these things ought not to be so.*

*(James 3:6-10)*

It defiles the whole body. It is a world of iniquity.
It is an unruly evil, full of deadly poison. How many
times have we been hurt by what our wives have
said? We can surely relate to what James is saying.
Most of us have been the recipient of our wives'
wrath and have been cut to the deep by their tongues.

But what about ourselves? What about our own
tongue? Are we guarding it?

*Whoever guards his mouth and tongue keeps his
soul from troubles.*

*(Proverbs 21:23)*

*He who guards his mouth preserves his life, But he who opens wide his lips shall have destruction.*

*(Proverbs 13:3)*

The ability to control the tongue is one of the clearest marks of wisdom. The tongue has the power of life and death.

*For"He who would love life and see good days, Let him refrain his tongue from evil, and his lips from speaking deceit.*

*(1 Peter 3:10)*

The scripture speaks loud and clear about our speech.

*Keep your tongue from evil, And your lips from speaking deceit.*

*(Psalm 34:13)*

I like James 1:26 (Paraphrased). You go to church every Sunday and you consider yourself religious. After service you gossip about everyone. Well, you have deceived yourself. Your religion is worthless.

*Let your speech always be with grace, seasoned with salt, that you may know how you ought to answer each one.*

*(Colossians 4:6)*

Let our conversations be always full of grace: Grace means favor, good will, kindness, a blessing, gratuity. Grace is also the power of God that enables us to perform the will of God.

There are so many ways that we do damage with our tongues: insults, ridicule, mocking, sarcasm, negatives. We do this especially to our wives and children and other members of our family, those we are supposed to be in authority over. If we are honest, we will admit, that much of the time, there is little grace in our conversations at home. Out of our frustrations we beat our families with our tongues. Sometimes we do it deliberately, verbally abusing anyone who gets in our way. Sometimes we take a more subtle approach and may not even realize we are doing it.

For example, when a man comes home from work expecting dinner to be ready, he finds his wife talking on the phone to her mother. Some of the comments might go like this; "Who are you talking to **this time**?" The **this time** makes her think that you think she is on the phone all day. "Doesn't she (her mother) realize what time it is?" Now you are telling her that you think her mother is inconsiderate. "After all, I have worked hard all day and all I have had to eat is that one sandwich you gave me for lunch." Now, she hears, that he has worked hard all day and thinks I have done nothing and that he hated the lunch I made him".

A wonderful start to the evening. Could ruin the whole week! We must think before we speak.

*He who has knowledge spares his words, and a man of understanding is of a calm spirit.*
*(Proverbs 17:27)*

This does not mean that we should not answer when we are spoken to or that we should not communicate. It is just the opposite.

The scripture says that our words should be:

## Pleasant:

*Pleasant words are like a honeycomb, sweetness to the soul and health to the bones.*
*(Proverbs 16:24)*

## Appropriate:

*A word fitly spoken is like apples of gold In settings of silver.*
*(Proverbs 25:11)*

## Gracious:

*The words of a wise man's mouth are gracious, But the lips of a fool shall swallow him up;*
*(Ecclesiastes 10:12)*

## Comforting:

*"The Lord GOD has given me the tongue of the learned, That I should know how to speak a word*

*in season to him who is weary. He awakens me*
*morning by morning, He awakens my ear To hear*
*as the learned.*

*(Isaiah 50:4)*

## Forceful:

*How forceful are right words! But what does your*
*arguing prove?*

*(Job 6:25)*

Jesus made a very strong statement about the heart and the tongue.

*A good man out of the good treasure of his heart*
*brings forth good; and an evil man out of the evil*
*treasure of his heart brings forth evil. For out of*
*the abundance of the heart his mouth speaks.*

*(Luke 6:45)*

What is in our hearts is what comes out of our mouths. That is why we have to feed the right things into our hearts. That is why we have to remove the plagued stones and get the garbage out of our lives. We have to fill our hearts with God, Jesus, the Holy Spirit. His way, His love. Pack into ourselves as much of Him as we can. The way we do this is by staying in the Word of God. The Word will chasten us, correct us, and reprove us. Then what we speak with our mouths will come from the abundance of our hearts, and will give glory to God.

*Let the words of my mouth and the meditation of my heart Be acceptable in Your sight, O LORD, my strength and my Redeemer.*

*(Psalm 19:14)*

*In the multitude of words sin is not lacking, but he who restrains his lips is wise.*

*(Proverbs 10:19)*

"To Restrain" is "to hold back, to check, to hold from action, to suppress, to limit, to confine." (Webster's 1828)

The tongue is the instrument that creates the sounds and words that come out of our mouths. We are the ones who play that instrument and we are the ones who control the sounds and the words that come out of it. When we are talking to our wives, our words should edify, our words should encourage, our words should comfort.

**Do not let any unwholesome talk come out of your mouths, but only what is helpful for building others up according to their needs, that it may benefit those who listen.**

**(Ephesians 4:29 NIV )**

# 11

## Love

Walter endures long and Walter is patient and Walter is kind, Walter never is envious, Walter never boils over with jealousy, Walter is not boastful or vain glorious, Walter does not display himself haughtily. Walter is not conceited, arrogant or inflated with pride, Walter is not rude, unmannerly and Walter does not act unbecomingly. Walter does not insist on his own rights or his own way, for Walter is not self seeking, Walter is not touchy or fretful or resentful, Walter takes no account of the evil done to him, Walter pays no attention to a suffered wrong. Walter does not rejoice at injustice and unrighteousness. But Walter rejoices when right and truth prevail. Walter bears up under anything and everything that comes, Walter is ever ready to believe the best of every person, Walter's hopes are fadeless under all circumstances, and Walter endures everything without weakening.

Wouldn't that be nice if that were all true. My home would be a perfect place to live if Walter were all those things. As you know, that was taken from 1 Cor.13 and all the places where you see my name, the word "LOVE" belongs. This is God's love! And we should put our own names in there. We, as born again Christians, have God's love in us. The world around us would change if we confessed these verses everyday with our own names in there and tried to live up to them.

I know that love is the answer to all our problems. Jesus bottom lined it in John 13:34:

*A new commandment I give to you, that you love one another; as I have loved you, that you also love one another.*

This is the message of Jesus, repeated all through the New Testament "Love one another."

Many years ago a priest friend of ours was visiting us in our home. It was a time in our lives when we were trying to deal with some issues regarding our children. This friend was staying for the weekend so we had a lot of time to talk, and talk I did. I dumped everything on him, and he listened intently. When I was through, I waited, expecting to receive some great words of wisdom from him or at least sympathy, but all he said was "Did you ever think of just loving them?" I ignored his question and it was many years before I realized he had given me great wisdom and that God had used him to solve my problem. Just love them with an agape love, an unconditional love.

God spared me from many things. He spared me from a broken home! My father and mother truly loved each other and lived very happily in their marriage, right up to their deaths. He spared me from a life of poverty! My needs have always been met. He spared me from alcohol and drugs. I've never had a problem with alcohol (at least not a serious problem), and I never even came close to drugs. He spared me from a life of crime! My worst crime was a speeding ticket. He spared me from a life of sexual immorality! The only woman I've ever known is the one I'm married to. God spared me from many things. But yet, I was as much of a sinner as anyone. I was like the Pharisees:

*"Two men went up to the temple to pray, one a Pharisee and the other a tax collector. [11] The Pharisee stood and prayed thus with himself, 'God, I thank You that I am not like other men — extortioners, unjust, adulterers, or even as this tax collector. [12] I fast twice a week; I give tithes of all that I possess.' [13] And the tax collector, standing afar off, would not so much as raise his eyes to heaven, but beat his breast, saying, 'God, be merciful to me a sinner!' [14] I tell you, this man went down to his house justified rather than the other; for everyone who exalts himself will be humbled, and he who humbles himself will be exalted."*

*(Luke 18:10-14)*

I thought I was righteous. That's what we should be, righteous. To be righteous is to be in right standing with God. But, I wasn't righteous. I was **self righteous.** The hardest person to win to the Lord is the self righteous one. We think we need no one but ourselves. Many of us who do turn to the Lord, do so thinking we will be able to help Him. We think that we are doing Him a favor.

Jesus tells Peter this story in Luke 7:40-47, about two men who owed a certain moneylender. One owed a lot of money and one not so much. Neither had the money to pay, so He canceled both debts. Jesus asked Peter "Which one will love him more?" Peter replied, "I suppose the one who had the bigger debt canceled." Jesus said "You have judged correctly." Then Jesus goes on and tells of the woman who washed His feet with her tears and wiped them with her hair. He tells how she kept kissing His feet and how she poured perfume on them. Then, Jesus said, "Therefore, I tell you, her **many** sins have been forgiven — for she loved much. But he who has been forgiven little loves little."

When you have done it all, and you think your life can go no lower, when you are desperate and you call out to God and He raises you up, and cleans you up and forgives you, then like the women in Luke 7, **you will have much love.**

The self righteous have no real love for anyone except for themselves. Jesus saved me from myself. He taught me how to love.

We live in a world that is removing God from everything. It is hard to believe that in such a short time God is no longer welcome in public places. The God of creation has been replaced by the mush god, the god of the world. The mush god lets you do whatever you want to do. "If it feels good, do it." That is the philosophy. There is no right or wrong with the mush god. It is just "Do it your way." The mush god is a god of self. A god who panders to the flesh.

When we give up the mush god and take on Jesus, we become God centered, God motivated. His interests become our interests. We want His will for our lives not our own. When we fill our hearts and our minds with His Word, when we yield ourselves completely to His Holy Spirit, our love takes on a new dimension. It is no longer "I", "I", "I". It becomes "Him," "His" and "He." Through our concentration on Him, the plagued stones leave one by one. We repent. We don't want them in our lives anymore. We are filled with love because we are filled with God. He becomes all to us. **He is Love!**

*He who does not love does not know God, for God is love.*

*(1 John 4:8)*

A lot of men are afraid of love. We are afraid it will make us look weak. We are afraid that if we are loving, we will be less than a man. We are afraid of how others will see us. Will they think we are wimps?

Jesus said, "Turn the other cheek." Jesus said, "If he takes your coat, give him your shirt." If you live this way, you will be men in the eyes of Jesus, and you will most likely look like a wimp to the eyes of the world.

I met a man who was a Colonel in the U.S. Marines. He had flown over three hundred combat missions and had a chest full of medals. When he gave his testimony, he dressed in his marine dress uniform. His boots were shined like glass and he was very impressive, standing there straight as an arrow. He talked about his combat missions and all the things he did to earn all those medals. Then he would say, "In the eyes of the U.S. Marine Corp. I am a hero, but in the eyes of God I am a zero hero." He would say "Flying planes in combat doesn't make you a man in the eyes of God. What makes you a man in the eyes of God is when you can walk up to another man, take his hand, look him straight in the eye and say, I love you, Brother and I care about you. That's a real man."

The world has perverted love, and what the

world calls love, God calls lust. What we see in movies and on television, and what we read in books and magazines have made lust and free sex seem okay. We even hear Christian men say there is no harm in looking. But there is! Serious harm!

*But I say to you that whoever looks at a woman to lust for her has already committed adultery with her in his heart.*

*(Matthew 5:28)*

In the movies and on the television, going to bed with someone is just a routine matter. We have fornication, adultery, and homosexuality blatantly and shamelessly fed to us. It has come to the point that anyone who speaks out against these actions is said to be discriminating or is told not to judge. God has already pre-judged these sins.

*Do you not know that the unrighteous will not inherit the kingdom of God? Do not be deceived. Neither fornicators, nor idolaters, nor adulterers, nor homosexuals, nor sodomites, [10] nor thieves, nor covetous, nor drunkards, nor revilers, nor extortioners will inherit the kingdom of God.*

*(1 Corinthians 6:9-10)*

We have been deceived and we have bought the lies of this world.

*For all that is in the world—the lust of the flesh, the lust of the eyes, and the pride of life—is not of*

94

*the Father but is of the world. [17] And the world*
*is passing away, and the lust of it; but he who does*
*the will of God abides forever.*

*(1 John 2:16-17)*

God has a better plan.

*But as it is written:"Eye has not seen, nor ear heard,*
*Nor have entered into the heart of man The things*
*which God has prepared for those who love Him."*

*(1 Corinthians 2:9)*

One of the major things that God has prepared
for us is marriage and the sexual relationship. God
designed the sexual relationship for the **husband
and the wife.** God created the sexual relationship.
It is a beautiful gift that He has given to married
couples. God created the woman and brought her
to the man. She was and is a special gift to him.
When couples have their roles in order, and they
come together under the unction of the Holy
Spirit, they will see what God has prepared for
those who love Him. Exceeding, abundantly, far
more than we could ask or imagine.

*Now to Him who is able to do exceedingly abun-*
*dantly above all that we ask or think, according to*
*the power that works in us,*

*(Ephesians 3:20)*

We should never enter into a time of physical
intimacy with our wives out of lust. She will never

be happy or satisfied and neither will you. A wife needs to be romanced and she needs for her husband to take leadership in this area. She doesn't want to feel that your love for her is just to fulfill a need. She wants to know in her heart that you love her unconditionally all the time.

The world, the flesh, and the devil have perverted God's special gift of married love. Couples, even Christian couples, are using all kinds of perverted methods to become sexually aroused (or turned on, as the world says). That is sick! It is proof of a diseased world. If you want to have times of sexual intimacy together with real meaning, seek the anointing of the Holy Spirit. Kneel together before the Lord, or just hold her in your arms in bed and ask the Lord to bless your time together. Talk about your relationship, her needs, and your needs. Then pray about them together. Be careful, this is not a time to discuss problems, kids, money etc. This is a time to concentrate on each other, a time to express your love and admiration for one another. A time to be open and free, to talk about your sexual needs and desires and to pray about them together. We, as the priests of our homes, should be the ones who instigate this time of prayer. God wants to be included in every facet of our lives. Don't leave Him out of this important area. You, your wife, and your relationship will be blessed beyond what you or your wife could ever comprehend. I've heard it said that, "Love is not the fulfilling of sexual desires, but sexual desires are fulfilled because of love."

What has happened? Why are so many couples, even Christian couples, separating and divorcing? One of the reasons is they have never truly become one.

*But from the beginning of the creation, God 'made them male and female.' [7] 'For this reason a man shall leave his father and mother and be joined to his wife, [8] and the two shall become one flesh'; so then they are no longer two, but one flesh. [9] Therefore what God has joined together, let not man separate."*
*(Mark 10:6-9)*

No man or woman in marriage can live or act independently of their spouse. If the two are one, there cannot be any areas of our lives where we can have a sign that says "Private, Husbands Only, Wives Keep Out." With the exception of God Himself, there can be no person or thing that comes before your wife.

The Amplified version of 1Peter 3:7 says: "Husbands, likewise dwell with them with under-standing, giving honor (to reverence; to manifest the highest veneration for, in words and action; to entertain the most exalted thoughts of; to worship; to adore.) to the wife, as the weaker vessel, and as being heirs together of the grace of life. That your prayers may not be hindered."

We must be committed to the role we have as the heads of our wives and accept and meet the challenge and responsibilities that God has given us. We are to be men like Jesus. We are to love our wives as Christ loved the church. We are to be the heads of our families. It is not easy, but it is the only way, and it means dying to self.

To Live, Die to Self

By

The Railroad Evangelist

When you're forgotten, or neglected, or purposely set aside, and you don't sting and hurt with the insult or oversight, but your heart is happy, being counted worthy to suffer for Christ, **that's dying to self**.

When your good is evil spoken of, when your wishes are crossed, your advice disregarded, your opinions ridiculed, and you refuse   to let anger rise in your heart, or even defend yourself, but you take it all in patient, loving silence, **that's dying to self.**

When you lovingly and patiently bear any disorder, any irregularity, any annoyance; when you stand face to face with waste, folly, extravagance, spiritual insensibility, and endure as Jesus endured, **that's dying to self.**

When you never care to refer to yourself in conversation, or to record your own good words, or itch after commendations, when you truly love to be unknown, **that's dying to self.**

When you can see your brother prosper and have his needs met and you can honestly rejoice with him and feel no envy, or question God, while your needs are far greater and in desperate circumstances, **that's dying to self.**

When you can receive correction and reproof from one of less stature than yourself and can humbly submit inwardly, as well as outwardly, finding no rebellion or resentment rising up within your heart, **that's dying to self.**

Are you dead yet? May the Spirit bring us to the cross. *(Phillipians 3:10) that I may know Him and the power of His resurrection, and the fellowship of His suffering, being conformed to His death.*

*Live joyfully with the wife whom you love all the days of your vain life which He has given you under the sun, all your days of vanity; for that is your portion in life, and in the labor which you perform under the sun.*

*(Ecclesiastes 9:9)*

We are to live joyfully with our wives and be the priests, prophets and kings of our families. It is our responsibly to see that the marriage not only works, but that it has all that God planned for it. It will take work on our part and sacrifice. It is so important for couples who are entering into marriage to understand their roles. The most important jobs in the world are those of husbands, wives, and parents. Very few people are trained or prepared for these positions. Most of us just jump into it.

Marriage is a life-long commitment. Marriages today either end up in divorce or the couple live their lives miserably unhappy. That is not God's plan. Some men look at their wives as their cross in life. Not so! If that is the case in your marriage or that is the direction that your marriage is heading, I have a bottom line for you. You are a wimp and chances are it is your fault. Marriage is commitment, marriage is sacrifice and marriage is work. If you put nothing into your marriage, you will get nothing out of it. **You will reap what you sow.** The world will try to tell you that after a period of time the honeymoon ends. Not so! The honeymoon should never end. We were meant to grow old together, happily.

*Love suffers long and is kind; love does not envy; love does not parade itself, is not puffed up; [5] does not behave rudely, does not seek its own, is not provoked, thinks no evil; [6] does not rejoice in iniquity, but rejoices in the truth; [7] bears all things, believes all things, hopes all things, endures all things. [8] Love never fails. But whether there are prophecies, they will fail; whether there are tongues, they will cease; whether there is knowledge, it will vanish away.*

*(1 Corinthians 13:4-8)*

# 12

## The "Be" Attitudes

Let us examine some of the areas in our marriages that we can improve on. Our attitudes can cause problems, and we need to be willing to look at them in the light of God's Word. We need to compare our attitudes with what the scriptures say our attitudes should be. I call them:

The "Be" Attitudes

**1. Be Happy** — Be fun to live with! If you had to choose one person to live with the rest of your life, would you choose you?

Joy is the second fruit of the Holy Spirit. Some of us bring as much joy into our homes as a skunk at a lawn party. Are our wives and children happy to see us come home?

*A cheerful look brings joy to the heart, and good news gives health to the bones.*

*(Proverbs 15:30 NIV)*

There are about 240 verses in the Bible that speak of being joyful and happy.

**2. Be Understanding** — When David prayed for Solomon in 1Chron. 22:12 NIV, he said: "May the Lord give you discretion and understanding when He puts you in command over our homes and families." "Understanding" is defined as, "The faculty of the human mind by which it apprehends the real state of things presented to it, or by which it receives or comprehends the ideas which others express and intend to communicate."(Webster's 1828) Being understanding doesn't mean giving up your authority or headship. It does mean taking the time to listen to someone else's point of view. I find it helpful to try to put myself in the other person's shoes, but in order to do that, I really have to listen.

**3. <u>Be</u> Compassionate** — "Compassionate" means "having a temper and or disposition to pity, inclined to show mercy, having a heart that is tender and easily moved by the distresses, sufferings, wants and weaknesses of others, having a loving attitude."

> *The LORD is gracious and full of compassion,*
> *Slow to anger and great in mercy.*
>
> *(Psalm 145:8)*

**4. <u>Be</u> Loyal** — Most of you would say you are loyal because you don't cheat on your wives. But there is another type of loyalty to consider. How do you talk about your wife? How do you talk about her to your friends, to your parents, to your children? I hear men talk about their wives, using "degrading, and vulgar curse words." They talk so disrespectfully about them and to them, and often times this happens in front of others. This should never be. You can tell they have never heard that their wives are "bone of their bones and flesh of their flesh."

*And Adam said: "This is now bone of my bones and flesh of my flesh; She shall be called Woman, because she was taken out of Man."*

*(Genesis 2:23)*

**5. <u>Be</u> Sympathetic** — After all, it is not easy living with us. Try to understand what your wife is going through. Many problems could be avoided if the husband would just reach out and say, "It's okay. I understand how you feel. I know you are going through a hard time. Don't worry. I will take care of everything." Remember, your wife goes through emotional changes every month. It is not always easy for her. Help her during these hard times. Think how you feel when **you** have a headache.

*For we do not have a High Priest who cannot sympathize with our weaknesses, but was in all points tempted as we are, yet without sin.*

*(Hebrews 4:15)*

*Finally, all of you be of one mind, having compassion for one another; love as brothers, be tenderhearted, be courteous;*

*(1 Peter 3:8)*

**6. <u>Be</u> Honest** — Don't lie to her. Again, most of us will say, "I never lie to my wife." But, are we honest with our thoughts and feelings? In order for a marriage to remain strong and continue to grow, a husband and wife need to communicate truth. Be willing to share your feelings, honestly and openly, putting down your pride and humbling yourself. A couple cannot have anything hidden if they are to have a successful marriage. Remember that God's Word says that both of you have become one:

> *... and the two shall become one flesh; so then they are no longer two, but one flesh.*
>
> *(Mark 10:8)*

**7. <u>Be</u> Patient** — Another fruit of the Holy Spirit. "Patience" is "having the quality of enduring evils without murmuring or fretfulness, having a calm unruffled temper."(Webster's 1828) When we are patient with our wives, it gives them time to hear from the Holy Spirit and to make corrections. Rather than getting resentful or rebellious towards us because of our negative attitudes, they have time to think things through and perhaps look at their own mistakes instead of ours. Jesus is always patient with us His Church, over which He has complete authority. Should we be any less patient with those over which we have authority?

*And a servant of the Lord must not quarrel but be
gentle to all, able to teach, patient,*

*(2 Tim. 2:24)*

*For the husband is head of the wife, as also Christ
is head of the church; and He is the Savior of the
body.*

*(Ephesians 5:23)*

**8. <u>Be</u> Kind** — Another fruit of the Holy Spirit.
"To be kind" means: "to do good to others and to
make them happy by granting their requests, sup-
plying their wants or assisting them in
distress."(Webster's 1828)

*And be kind to one another, tenderhearted, forgiv-
ing one another, just as God in Christ forgave you.*
*(Ephesians 4:32)*

**9. <u>Be</u> Loving** — Most men think of love in
association with the bedroom. That is wrong. If a
wife only experiences love and tenderness as a
build up towards sex, then she may well feel that
is the only time she is truly loved and she may
become withdrawn and resentful. If we love our
wives the way that God wants us to love them,
then the sexual part of our relationship will take
care of itself. The important question is how do we
show our love to our wives the rest of the time?
Our wives were given to us by God. Therefore we
should put them before all else in the world.

105

Our wives should come before our parents.
Our wives should come before our children.
Our wives should come before our jobs or businesses.
Our wives should come before our friends.
Our wives should come before our sports.
Our wives should come before our ministries.

Our wives should come before anything else that might interest us . Tell her often that you love and appreciate her. Kiss her for no particular reason. Hold her hand. Nothing tells her that you love her any more than an outward display of affection **with no strings attached.**

*Husbands, love your wives, just as Christ also loved the church and gave Himself for her ...*
*(Ephesians 5:25)*

**10. <u>Be</u> Courteous** — "To be courteous" means "to be polite, well bred, being of elegant manners, civil, obliging."(Webster's 1828) Most of us will use these traits with everyone except our own wives. Be courteous at meal time, as if you were eating in a restaurant. Don't just grab the food and shovel it in. Don't leave the table before she's finished. Don't watch television or read the paper, while you are eating. Treat her like a well respected friend.

*Finally, all of you be of one mind, having compassion for one another; love as brothers, be tenderhearted, be courteous;*

*(1 Peter 3:8)*

**11. Be Caring** — "To be caring" means "to be concerned." (Webster's 1828) It is important to express concern, to really listen to what your wife has to say and to participate in conversation with her. When you come home at night, ask her how her day went. When she starts to tell you, don't make thoughtless statements like: "I don't know why you feel like that." "That is really stupid, just forget it." "You spoil everything when you get like this." "I hope you are not going to bring that up again." Sometimes all she really wants is **you**, to listen and to care.

One time I came home and Gene was having a really bad day. She was very upset. I asked her what it was all about. When she saw that perhaps I was truly interested, she eagerly began to share it with me. The old me would have picked up the mail and looked through it while she talked, or grabbed the newspaper and glanced through it while interjecting, "Uh huh," every once in awhile. Or I might have clicked on the television with one ear cocked to what she was saying. But this time, by the grace of God, I didn't regress into that old, familiar insensitive behavior. Instead, I made a decision to listen. I sat down with her, looked right at her, and gave her my full attention. Most of what was bothering her was not what I call "men things." It would have been really easy to say the usual "You shouldn't feel that way" and then gone about my business. As I listened I began to feel her pain and began to really understand how she was feeling. (Feelings are neither right nor wrong; they just are). She talked until 11P.M. Now, remember these were not issues regarding money or children, but these were her feelings about many situations, some that went back into her childhood. They were important to her, and she needed me to listen. She didn't need advice; she just needed me to listen. The next morning as I was getting ready to leave, Gene came to me. Her whole countenance was different. She seemed free. She put her arms around me, kissed me, and said, "Thanks. You helped me so much last night. I feel like a new person." What did I do? I listened. I was concerned for what was concerning her. And I know my wife better, because of it.

*Let each of you look out not only for his own inter-*
*ests, but also for the interests of others. [5] Let this*
*mind be in you which was also in Christ Jesus ...*
*(Philippians 2:4-5)*

**12. <u>Be</u> Strong** — Women need their husbands to be strong, not just in physical strength. As the heads of our homes sometimes God calls us to make difficult decisions that might even seem at first glance to be wrong. Be strong. Don't buckle under pressure. I remember one time that I had to make a decision that involved one of our children. It was a very hard time in his life. Emotionally and physically, he was at an all time low. I felt (after much prayer) that I had to ask him to move out. Sometimes tough love is necessary. I received a lot of flack from all directions. I even had scripture quoted to me (especially from my wife). But, I felt very strong about this, and I stood my ground. It turned out that moving out was the right thing for him and for the rest of the family. A woman who understands submission experiences great liberation when her husband takes full charge and responsibility in difficult situations through the direction of the Lord.

*Finally, my brethren, be strong in the Lord and in the power of His might.*

*(Ephesians 6:10)*

**13. <u>Be</u> Firm** — Sometimes it is hard to make a decision and then to stick to it, particularly if your wife does not know the Lord or does not understand the things of the Spirit. It is wise not to make decisions too quickly. Listen to all the ideas and opinions of others. Do your homework. Then take all the time you need to pray and seek the Lord. In this way you will not be making snap decisions in the flesh that could end up being very costly. When you are sure you have heard from the Lord, and you have His Word to confirm it, then act on it and stick to it. Be steady.

*But let your 'Yes' be 'Yes,' and your 'No,' 'No.' For whatever is more than these is from the evil one.*
*(Matthew 5:37)*

**14. <u>Be</u> Diligent** — This is the cry of many wives. "He starts everything but finishes nothing."

*The soul of a lazy man desires, and has nothing;*
*But the soul of the diligent shall be made rich.*
*(Proverbs 13:4)*

"Diligent" means "steady in application, constant in effort or exertion to accomplish what is undertaken".(Webster's 1828)

**15. <u>Be</u> Forgiving** — We shouldn't hold any unforgiveness towards anyone, for any reason, no matter what he or she has done or said. Do we not expect God to forgive us for everything we have done or said? Can we do any less? Unforgiveness is a hindrance. No, it is worse than a hindrance. It is an obstruction to our walk with the Lord and to our relationships with others. It keeps us from getting our prayers answered. We can't be a loving caring person like Jesus unless we forgive as He forgives. Forgiving is not saying, "I forgive that person, but I'm just not going to have anything to do with him or her." We have to forgive from our hearts, and then forget about it. Don't say "I cannot do that" because you can. Just as you make up your mind not to forgive a person, you can make up your mind **to** forgive a person.

> *"And whenever you stand praying, if you have anything against anyone, forgive him, that your Father in heaven may also forgive you your trespasses. [26] But if you do not forgive, neither will your Father in heaven forgive your trespasses."*
> *(Mark 11:25-26)*

> *For You, Lord, are good, and ready to forgive, and abundant in mercy to all those who call upon You.*
> *(Psalm 86:5)*

> *And be kind to one another, tenderhearted, forgiving one another, just as God in Christ forgave you.*
> *(Ephesians 4:32)*

**16. Be Accepting** — It is easy to accept the "behavior" we like and even the "behavior" we do not mind. But try to accept some of the "behavior" you do not like, the "behavior" that is an irritation to you. Gene used to cry when she was upset, and it really irritated me. My comments would be, "What's the matter, now? What are you crying about? You are spoiling everything." It always seemed to me that she would cry at the most inappropriate times. One day I just gave her a hug and told her it was okay. I said "Go ahead and cry. Let the tears wash away the hurts." Guess what? She hardly ever cries anymore.

*Rejoice with those who rejoice, and weep with those who weep.*

*(Romans. 12:15)*

### 17. Be Wise —

*If any of you lacks wisdom, let him ask of God, who gives to all liberally and without reproach, and it will be given to him.*

*(James 1:5)*

A wise man is the one who has the power to discern and judge correctly.

*But the wisdom that is from above is first pure, then peaceable, gentle, willing to yield, full of mercy and good fruits, without partiality and without hypocrisy.*

*(James 3:17)*

This is the wisdom we need in order to provide headship to our families. Wisdom that is peaceable, gentle, willing to yield, full of mercy. We will never get this kind of wisdom from the world; we get it only from God.

*Because the foolishness of God is wiser than men, and the weakness of God is stronger than men.*
*(Corinthians 1:25)*

**18. Be Appreciative** — When you come into your home and your dinner is prepared for you, your children are well cared for and the house is neat and clean, make sure to express to your wife how much you appreciate what she does. And understand when it's not that way. Perhaps she has been working all day to help you support the family financially. Tell her how much you appreciate that, and ask her if there is something you can do to lighten her load. Look for things to compliment her on, rather than things to complain about.

*Let no corrupt word proceed out of your mouth, but what is good for necessary edification, that it may impart grace to the hearers.*
*(Ephesians 4:29)*

**19. Be Friendly** — Think about how you greet your friends and how you treat them. I see so many couples who are constantly complaining about each other (to anybody who will listen). They are always competing with each other, blaming each other, and making snide remarks. You can see that they look at each other as if they were enemies rather than the

113

"one" that they are according to God's Word. They strive to be separate and maintain an individuality that is a detriment to their marriage. All of your wife's talents, all of her skills, all of her abilities are yours. All of your talents, all of your skills, all of your abilities are hers. This is the way God designed it. We get a double portion when we marry. Instead of fighting against each other and competing with each other, let us work together as one. My wife is my best friend

> *So husbands ought to love their own wives as their own bodies; he who loves his wife loves himself.*
> *(Ephesians 5:28)*

**20. Be Encouraging** — "To encourage" means "to give or to increase confidence". (Webster's 1828) We men get the mistaken idea that we are the only ones doing anything worthwhile. We look on the women's role as secondary to ours (and it is, in the sense that we are the head and they are, or should be dependent upon us). But, everything that they are called to do is important, especially to us. They make us look good. Their support and encouragement is vital to our success and well being. We should become aware of what our wives are trying to accomplish and encourage them in that.

*Therefore encourage (admonish, exhort) one another and edify (strengthen and build up) one another, just as you are doing.*
*(1 Thessalonians 5:11 Amplified)*

**21. Be Gentle** — Gentleness is another fruit of the Holy Spirit. Be a gentle man. Women love gentleness. The uncouth, rough, foul- mouthed man, may have a life in the movies, but there is no place for that man in a marriage. Jesus is a gentle man.

*Take My yoke upon you and learn from Me, for I am gentle and lowly in heart, and you will find rest for your souls. [30] For My yoke is easy and My burden is light."*
*(Matthew 11:29-30)*

**22. Be Desirable** — Should the idea of being desirable apply only to women?

*Now the works of the flesh are evident, which are: adultery, fornication, uncleanness, lewdness ...*
*(Galatians 5:19)*

The works of the flesh are evident: adultery, fornication, and **uncleanness**. The Word means exactly what it says. Keeping or allowing yourself to be unclean is a work of the flesh. Did you ever go to give your wife a hug and she backed up five paces? How is your breath? How is your deodorant? How are your whiskers? How is your hair? It is a simple matter to keep yourself well groomed and appealing to your wife. Remember how you prepared yourself before you were married?

**23. <u>Be</u> Reasonable** — Your wife is not your slave, nor are you a slave driver. Give her space. Don't complain when she wants time with friends or relatives, or when she wants to talk on the phone. Some women love to talk. We are inclined to think they go over and over the same things. But we need to accept them the way they are. Don't demand your wife's attention every minute that you are around. You are the head of the home. You are not running a dictatorship.

> *He who has knowledge spares his words, and a man of understanding has a cool spirit.*
> > *(Proverbs 17:27 Amplified)*

**24. <u>Be</u> Thankful** — We do not seem to have any trouble finding things to murmur and complain about, but we are not too quick to give thanks.

> *In everything give thanks; for this is the will of God in Christ Jesus for you.*
> > *(1Thessalonians 5:18)*

We say, "Oh! If I only knew what God's will is for me." Well, you **<u>do</u>** know. We just read it in 1 Thes. 5:18. "In <u>everything</u> give thanks." "Oh! but you don't know **my** circumstances." Give thanks for the circumstances because growth often comes in the midst of the circumstances. If you have committed your life to Jesus, and He is running your life, and He has said, "I will never leave you or forsake you" (Heb.13:5), then trust His Word and keep on being thankful. The attitudes that you as the head bring into the home are contagious. If **you** are thankful, so will your wife and family be thankful.

### 25. <u>Be</u> Considerate —

*Love suffers long and is kind; love does not envy; love does not parade itself, is not puffed up; [5] does not behave rudely, does not seek its own, is not provoked, thinks no evil;*

*(1Corinthians 13:4-5)*

Love does not demand its own way. When her wishes do not conflict with what God is telling you, put her desires before yours. Back to dying to self. Don't drive too fast if it makes her nervous. Help around the house when you can. Pick up your own clothes. If she likes the crusty end of the bread give it to her. Once in awhile ask her if there is something she would like to have or someplace she would really like to go. Go with her <u>willingly</u>.

**26. <u>Be</u> One** — The Bible says in Eph.5:28, that we should love our wives as we love our own bodies. We protect our own bodies, and we need to protect our wives. We should keep them covered with prayer constantly. Praying with our wives is something we men seem to have a difficult time doing. But it is very important! The couple that prays together will be much closer, not only to each other but also to the Lord. I'm not talking about just saying grace before meals. I'm talking about quality time praying together. Doing this every day would be the ideal situation, but maybe that's not possible or even necessary in your case. Praying together once or twice a week just to praise and thank the Lord would be a plus in any relationship. Make your prayers, prayers of thanks.

*Giving thanks always for all things to God the Father in the name of our Lord Jesus Christ,*
*(Ephesians 5:20)*

Thank Him for your life; thank Him for your wife; thank Him for your children; thank Him for the new day; thank Him for your home; thank Him for your finances; and that He meets all your needs. Thank Him for your health; thank Him for your job or business. Most of all thank Him for salvation and for the mighty work He is doing in you. Then pray for your relatives and friends. Pray for the areas of your life and your marriage that need improvement. If you two are going to become one, then you must each be willing to do whatever is necessary to get rid of all hostilities and misunderstandings. Division is the name of an insidious game that the devil loves to play. Be one in Jesus, in church, in business, in fun, in sorrow, in failures, in successes.

*Therefore what God has joined together, let not man separate.*

*(Mark 10:9)*

Our wives need to be understood. There has to be communication between husbands and wives. Communication only comes about when there is understanding of the meaning of our words to each other. If you don't understand what a person is saying or what he or she means or what he or she is feeling, then there is no communication. Our wives need to feel secure and safe. Our wives need to feel affection: "Affection" is defined as "that state of being loved, feeling that unexplainable warmth inside". (Webster's 1828) Our wives need to feel essential, important to the highest degree.

Our first priority should be our homes if we are husbands and fathers. **If what you have does not work at home, then don't export it.** I know of men who are in the ministry, and their homes are a mess.

# 13

# One Little Rose

*Husbands, likewise, dwell with them with under-*
*standing, giving honor to the wife, as to the weaker*
*vessel, and as being heirs together of the grace of*
*life, that your prayers may not be hindered.*

*(1 Peter 3:7)*

"To hinder" means: "to stop, to interrupt, to obstruct, to prevent from moving forward by any means." (Webster's 1828)

I like the way 1 Peter 3:7 reads in the Living Bible "and if you don't treat her as you should, your prayers will not get ready answers."

I have heard it said so many times, "God doesn't answer my prayers." Then, maybe it's time for you to check out how you are treating your wife.

A wife wants to be cherished, protected, and treated special. This is her nature — the God-given desire of her heart. At the same time, she does not want to be given into, or have the headship and authority given over to her. Wives who have taken over the headship in their homes have no respect for their husbands. Wives instinctively know that the roles are reversed. The fact that their husbands will not do their parts is a constant irritation to them. A wife wants a strong, kind husband — not one who tries to whip everyone into shape with a loud voice, screaming and using harsh and hurting words. If I am describing you, then you are a wimp. A wife wants a husband who will lead and take over the headship of the home with gentle firmness, that is full of love and consideration for her and their children.

She wants guidelines, but she needs to be given freedom within those guidelines. Don't try to run everything. Give her authority to keep the house, but don't check up on every little thing she does. Don't haunt her. If things are not being taken care of the way you think they should be, tell her kindly what you expect, but don't put her through a white glove inspection.

Regarding money, you are the one who should make the budget and set the guidelines. Talk over with her what she thinks she needs for groceries, clothing, and household expenses. Work with her, consider her input but you make the final decision. Be sure to give her plenty of freedom within the budget on which you decide.

Regarding home decorating, let her do it her way. She is the homemaker, and it is important for her to be creative there. Work with her; give her suggestions; let her know what you like; but give her freedom.

Regarding parenting, it is very important for you to explain to your wife what you expect from her in this area. Help her to understand that you are the one responsible for the family. Help her to see that you are the one responsible before God for setting the rules and regulations. Help her to understand that her role is to carry them out according to your instructions.

These things may seem minor and insignificant to many of you. But they are not. They are important. The point is that you have to be involved as the head of the home in every area. When it is established that you are the head and that you are interested in everything that goes on in your marriage and in your home, you will find it a lot easier for both of you to walk in the roles God designed for you.

A wife loves what is now called old-fashioned treatment. But it never really goes out of style. Things like:

1. Being asked out on a date.
2. Having the car door opened for her.
3. Being seated first.
4. Not being left in a crowd while you are off talking to others.
5. Being driven places.
6. Lugging the groceries in for her.

7. Doing heavy work around the house.

8. Being called when you expect to be late.

9. Bringing home an unexpected gift or flowers.

10. Calling up, just to say "Hi."

11. Lots of hugs, just for nothing.

12. Being treated nicely, even when she is acting badly.

13. Really listening when she is having a bad time without putting condemnation on her.

Men, consider carefully the following: When a couple get married, the man doesn't give up anything? As a matter of fact he gains something precious, "A helpmate."

On the other hand a woman gives up much. She gives up her name. She marries into you, into your family. She is required to come into submission. "Submission" is defined as "coming under the authority of another without murmuring or complaining."(Webster's 1828) It means "doing something you do not want to do", or "not being able to do something you want to do." This is difficult for her. If you want to do it, that is not submission; that is agreement. Be sympathetic and understanding, but do not give up your authority.

Pray for God to show you your wife's heart. Pray for God to show you what her likes and dislikes are, what makes her happy and what hurts her. Don't assume you already know. Pray that you will understand her sensitive spirit, and that you will be strong enough not to give in to her. Help her to deal with these sensitive areas by talking with her, taking authority in prayer and finding out together what the mind of God is in the situation. She will then be happy to submit to your authority.

And, do not think a date has to be a $45.00 dinner. Just a ride in the car and a cup of coffee, or a walk, holding hands on the beach, or downtown, listening to her and communicating with her the whole time. This is romance. After a few of these dates, you might find that you will both feel much closer, and your marriage will be much richer. And do not think you have to buy her expensive gifts or send her huge bouquets of flowers. Sometimes just,

## *"One little rose will say it all."*

# 14

## Accountability — Responsibility — Commitment

God's principles of accountability, responsibility, and commitment can be found throughout the Bible in both the Old and the New Testaments.

When we study about the Israelite's journey in the Old Testament, and we study the prophets, and Paul's letters, and the letters of the other apostles and disciples in the New Testament, we can clearly see that our relationship to God is not a one way street.

*But he who did not know, yet committed things deserving of stripes, shall be beaten with few. For everyone to whom much is given, from him much will be required; and to whom much has been committed, of him they will ask the more.*

*(Luke 12:48)*

I don't think that there are too many people here in the United States who lack for much. We are going to be held accountable for everything that God has given us. Read the parable of the talents in Matthew 25. God has given us so much, and we carelessly have squandered much of it. I'm not just referring to money. We have been given many gifts: Living in the United States of

America, having the freedom to share what we know about God with others, the freedom to study His ways and practice them in our lives, the freedom to train our children in the way they should go. We will be held accountable for the way in which we have used what He has given us.

We pray and ask God for wisdom (and rightly so), but we are responsible for all the wisdom and knowledge that He gives us. We are responsible for resisting the enemy and for standing up for the standards of God. He has equipped us to fulfill this responsibility everywhere, everyday.

*Finally, my brethren, be strong in the Lord and in the power of His might. [11] Put on the whole armor of God, that you may be able to stand against the wiles of the devil. [12] For we do not wrestle against flesh and blood, but against principalities, against powers, against the rulers of the darkness of this age, against spiritual hosts of wickedness in the heavenly places. [13] Therefore take up the whole armor of God, that you may be able to withstand in the evil day, and having done all, to stand. [14] Stand therefore, having girded your waist with truth, having put on the breastplate of righteousness,*

*(Ephesians 6:10-14)*

The day of evil is here, yet we are not fulfilling our responsibility to stand for righteousness. There is no lukewarm with God.

*So then, because you are lukewarm, and neither cold nor hot, I will vomit you out of My mouth.*

*(Revelation 3:16)*

There is no middle ground, only right versus wrong, good versus evil and light versus darkness. We will either stand our ground or lose ground, conquer or be conquered, stand or fall. Riding the fence is not acceptable. We are counted among the forces on one side or the other.

Back in Genesis we see that man made a choice, and sin entered the world. Man could not pay the debt for that sin. So, Jesus came and paid the debt that we could not pay. Jesus paid our debt and when someone pays your debt, you are held accountable to that person. You owe him something.

*How can I repay the LORD for all his goodness to me?*

*(Psalm 116:12 NIV)*

*... you were bought at a price. Therefore honor God with your body.*

*(1 Corinthians 6:20 NIV)*

These scriptures also show us that we will be held accountable.

*Therefore the kingdom of heaven is like a certain king who wanted to settle accounts with his servants.*

*(Matthew 18:23)*

*But I say to you that for every idle word men may speak, they will give account of it in the day of judgment.*

*(Matthew 12:36)*

*But God said to him, 'Fool! This night your soul will be required of you; then whose will those things be which you have provided?'*

*(Luke 12:20)*

*So then each of us shall give account of himself to God.*

*(Romans 14:12)*

*They will give an account to Him who is ready to judge the living and the dead.*

*(1 Peter 4:5)*

We have been given much, and much will be expected. This is a heavy word — responsibility — accountability. They are not popular subjects, especially in today's society of "I Did It My Way." Whether we believe this or not does not change the fact that God said it and means it. We will still be held responsible for what God has given us, and we will be called to give an account. There is no way around it. You may say "This is too much for me; the world is always pulling me in the other direction." That might be true. But the world and the flesh will always try to pull us away from the truths of God and His Word. This is part and parcel of our life. Let us look at God's answer (one of many) to this dilemma. We find His answer in Isaiah 26:2-4 (Amplified Bible).

*Open the gates, that the [uncompromisingly] righteous nation which keeps her faith and her troth [with God] may enter in. (Troth means one's pledged word (Webster's 1828). You will guard him and keep him in perfect and constant peace whose mind [both its inclination and its character] is stayed on You, because he commits himself to You, leans on You, and hopes confidently in You. So, trust in the Lord (commit yourself to Him, lean on Him, hope confidently in Him) forever; for the Lord God is an everlasting Rock [the Rock of Ages].*

The key here is to commit yourself to Him. "To commit" means, "to send to or upon, to throw, put or lay upon, to give in trust, to put into the hands or power of another, to entrust to. Commit thy way to the Lord. (Ps 37:5) The things thou hast heard of me, commit to faithful men. (2 Timothy 2:2)."(Webster's 1828) Commitment is the key to becoming a man like Jesus. When we make marriage vows, we are committing ourselves to God and to our wives. Commitment is being faithful to those vows, no matter what. It means not quitting when the going gets rough. It means not using someone else's negative behavior as an excuse to back away from the vows we made. Jesus committed Himself to crucifixion (the ultimate commitment). Jesus could have said, "These ungrateful people are not worth this", and backed away from His commitment. Like the husband who quits because his wife will not co-operate and gives his authority and responsibility over to her. Or a father who gives up on his child because of the child's rebellion or bad attitude.

Commit yourself to the Lord!
Commit yourself to obeying His Word!
Commit yourself to be used in whatever way He sees fit.

Satan and the demonic forces under his command, are constantly trying to pull us away from God. That is their job and they are good at it. But God is greater than principalities and powers and rulers of darkness and spiritual wickedness in high places.

*But from there you will seek the LORD your God, and you will find Him if you seek Him with all your heart and with all your soul.*

*(Deuteronomy 4:29)*

This is what it is all about: seek Him and you **will** be:

The man God wants you to be.
The husband God wants you to be.
The father God wants you to be.
The head of the home that God wants you to be.

# 15

## Abide

In the beginning God spoke directly with man face to face. We find a lot of that type of communication in Genesis. Adam walked with God and talked with God as did Moses and Abraham. Then God spoke to man through the prophets and angels in dreams and visions. And then God established a new means of communication for us. Through Jesus! By using His name we have access to the Father.

Into each man God put a brain. It is a two-way communication system intricately connected to every part of the body. And beyond the brain, deeper into man, is a part of man that is more powerful, more of a master of this created tent (us) than the brain. It is the real, the everlasting man, the spirit of man. In its healthy state this spirit is controlled by the Holy Spirit, God's Spirit. This is why a man must be born again, born of the Holy Spirit, where he takes on the nature of God.

About 2000 years ago somewhere in Jerusalem, on a day called Pentecost, there were gathered together a group of men and women. These men and women witnessed one of the greatest gifts ever given to mankind. They witnessed the Holy Spirit make His entrance into the world. First, came a sound from heaven, like the rushing of a mighty wind and it filled the room. Then, tongues of fire danced around the room and fell on each one of them. It must have been an awesome experience to witness all that. They were most likely afraid and maybe a little anxious. But as He filled the room with His Presence, they wanted to drink Him in; they wanted to be filled by Him. The more they drank Him in the more power they felt in their bodies. This is what we are blessed to have in the world today. We just have to receive Him. Every time a man or a woman makes a commitment to Jesus, the Holy Spirit begins His work. The same power that shaped the universe and that created mankind, comes and lives in us. The same Spirit that raised Jesus from the dead comes and resides in us.

The Bible tells us that you and I can have enough of the Holy Spirit's power in us to do greater works than Jesus did.

> *"Most assuredly, I say to you, he who believes in Me, the works that I do he will do also; and greater works than these he will do, because I go to My Father."*
>
> *(John 14:12)*

Or you and I can be satisfied with the status quo. Be vigilant, however. There will come a time when the Holy Spirit will leave.

*For the mystery of lawlessness is already at work; only He who now restrains will do so until He is taken out of the way.*

*(2 Thessalonians 2:7)*

I believe we will go with Him. But, while we are here, and while He is here, let us receive all that He has for us.

*And I will pray the Father, and He will give you another Helper, that He may abide with you forever — [17] the Spirit of truth, whom the world cannot receive, because it neither sees Him nor knows Him; but you know Him, for He dwells with you and will be in you.*

*(John 14:16-17)*

*However, when He, the Spirit of truth, has come, He will guide you into all truth; for He will not speak on His own authority, but whatever He hears He will speak; and He will tell you things to come.*

*(John 16:13)*

## It is He who Regenerates us:

*Jesus answered and said to him, "Most assuredly, I say to you, unless one is born again, he cannot see the kingdom of God." [4] Nicodemus said to Him, "How can a man be born when he is old? Can he enter a second time into his mother's womb and be born?" [5] Jesus answered, "Most assuredly, I say*

*to you, unless one is born of water and the Spirit,
he cannot enter the kingdom of God.*

*(John 3:3-5)*

Regenerates means to change from a natural to a spiritual state. (Webster's 1828)

## It is He who Indwells us:

*But if the Spirit of Him who raised Jesus from the
dead dwells in you, He who raised Christ from the
dead will also give life to your mortal bodies
through His Spirit who dwells in you.*

*(Romans 8:11)*

## It is He who Anoints us:

*But you have an anointing from the Holy One, and
you know all things.*

*(1 John 2:20)*

*But the anointing which you have received from Him
abides in you, and you do not need that anyone
teach you; but as the same anointing teaches you
concerning all things, and is true, and is not a lie,
and just as it has taught you, you will abide in Him.*

*(1 John 2:27)*

## It is He who Baptizes us:

*Then Peter said to them, "Repent, and let every one
of you be baptized in the name of Jesus Christ for*

134

*the remission of sins; and you shall receive the gift of the Holy Spirit. [39] For the promise is to you and to your children, and to all who are afar off, as many as the Lord our God will call." [40] And with many other words he testified and exhorted them, saying, "Be saved from this perverse generation." [41] Then those who gladly received his word were baptized; and that day about three thousand souls were added to them.*

*(Acts 2:38-41)*

## It is He who Guides us:

*However, when He, the Spirit of truth, has come, He will guide you into all truth; for He will not speak on His own authority, but whatever He hears He will speak; and He will tell you things to come.*

*(John 16:13)*

## It is He who Sanctifies us:

*... that I might be a minister of Jesus Christ to the Gentiles, ministering the gospel of God, that the offering of the Gentiles might be acceptable, sanctified by the Holy Spirit.*

*(Romans 15:16)*

"To sanctify" means "to cleanse, purify or make holy, to separate." (Webster's 1828)

## It is He who Comforts us:

*And I will pray the Father, and He will give you another Helper, that He may abide with you forever — [17]*

135

*the Spirit of truth, whom the world cannot receive, because it neither sees Him nor knows Him; but you know Him, for He dwells with you and will be in you. [18] I will not leave you orphans; I will come to you. [19] "A little while longer and the world will see Me no more, but you will see Me. Because I live, you will live also. [20] At that day you will know that I am in My Father, and you in Me, and I in you. [21] He who has My commandments and keeps them, it is he who loves Me. And he who loves Me will be loved by My Father, and I will love him and manifest Myself to him." [22] Judas (not Iscariot) said to Him, "Lord, how is it that You will manifest Yourself to us, and not to the world?" [23] Jesus answered and said to him, "If anyone loves Me, he will keep My word; and My Father will love him, and We will come to him and make Our home with him. [24] He who does not love Me does not keep My words; and the word which you hear is not Mine but the Father's who sent Me. [25] "These things I have spoken to you while being present with you. [26] But the Helper, the Holy Spirit, whom the Father will send in My name, He will teach you all things, and bring to your remembrance all things that I said to you.*

*(John 14:16-26)*

## It is He who gives us Joy:

*... for the kingdom of God is not eating and drinking, but righteousness and peace and joy in the Holy Spirit.*

*(Romans 14:17)*

# It is He who gives us Discernment:

*But God has revealed them to us through His Spirit. For the Spirit searches all things, yes, the deep things of God. [11] For what man knows the things of a man except the spirit of the man which is in him? Even so no one knows the things of God except the Spirit of God. [12] Now we have received, not the spirit of the world, but the Spirit who is from God, that we might know the things that have been freely given to us by God. [13] These things we also speak, not in words which man's wisdom teaches but which the Holy Spirit teaches, comparing spiritual things with spiritual. [14] But the natural man does not receive the things of the Spirit of God, for they are foolishness to him; nor can he know them, because they are spiritually discerned. [15] But he who is spiritual judges all things, yet he himself is rightly judged by no one. [16] For "who has known the mind of the LORD that he may instruct Him?" But we have the mind of Christ.*

*(1 Corinthians 2:10-16)*

# It is He who bears Fruit:

*But the fruit of the Spirit is love, joy, peace, long suffering, kindness, goodness, faithfulness, [23] gentleness, self-control. Against such there is no law.*
*(Galatians 5:22-23)*

## It is He who gives Gifts:

*But the manifestation of the Spirit is given to each one for the profit of all: [8] for to one is given the word of wisdom through the Spirit, to another the word of knowledge through the same Spirit, [9] to another faith by the same Spirit, to another gifts of healings by the same Spirit, [10] to another the working of miracles, to another prophecy, to another discerning of spirits, to another different kinds of tongues, to another the interpretation of tongues. [11] But one and the same Spirit works all these things, distributing to each one individually as He wills.*

*(1 Corinthians 12:7-11)*

All the ingredients we need to be the husbands, fathers and heads of our homes.

He is eternal, omnipotent (all powerful), omniscient (all knowing), omnipresent (everywhere). He communicates with our spirit. He lives in each one of us, in each born-again believer. It says in James 4:8, "Draw near to God, and He will draw near to you." We must read His Word; we must meditate on Him day and night; we must abide in Him; we must believe in Him; we must trust Him; we must drink Him in.

*On the last day, that great day of the feast, Jesus stood and cried out, saying, "If anyone thirsts, let him come to Me and drink. [38] He who believes in*

*Me, as the Scripture has said, out of his heart will flow rivers of living water."*

*(John 7:37-38)*

We receive the Holy Spirit, and we are on fire. We get the power and we get filled, but we "leak" and we do nothing to get the power back.

It's much like an automobile battery. When you purchase a new battery, the first thing the mechanic does is fill it with fluid, then he puts it on a charger; then he puts it into the automobile. You then have a new power filled battery. This new battery will start your car, run your head lights, radio, heater, windshield wipers, electric locks, your clock etc. If the battery is simply put into the car and is just hooked up to the equipment that needs electrical power, then it is soon going to run out of power. The generator is the power source for the battery. It puts the power back into the battery. This is the power that all the other sources have drawn out. When the power of the Holy Spirit is drawn out of us by circumstances, trials and tribulations, then we need a generator to put that power back in. **The Word of God is our generator.**

The breath of life was breathed into us from God's own lips.

*And the LORD God formed man of the dust of the ground, and breathed into his nostrils the breath of life; and man became a living being.*

*(Genesis 2:7)*

The Spirit which God breathed into man is what causes us to seek after the things of God. But the temptations of the flesh are many and man's spirit is weak and he cannot do it on his own. The human mind wants to please the human body and give it its desires. That's why God gave us His Holy Spirit, to live in us, to direct us, to comfort and lead us.

*There is therefore now no condemnation to those who are in Christ Jesus, who do not walk according to the flesh, but according to the Spirit. [2] For the law of the Spirit of life in Christ Jesus has made me free from the law of sin and death. [3] For what the law could not do in that it was weak through the flesh, God did by sending His own Son in the likeness of sinful flesh, on account of sin: He condemned sin in the flesh, [4] that the righteous requirement of the law might be fulfilled in us who do not walk according to the flesh but according to the Spirit. [5] For those who live according to the flesh set their minds on the things of the flesh, but those who live according to the Spirit, the things of the Spirit. [6] For to be carnally minded is death, but to be spiritually minded is life and peace. [7] Because the carnal mind is enmity against God; for it is not subject to the law of God, nor indeed can be. [8] So then, those who are in the flesh cannot please God. [9] But you are not in the flesh but in*

*the Spirit, if indeed the Spirit of God dwells in you.
Now if anyone does not have the Spirit of Christ, he
is not His. [10] And if Christ is in you, the body is
dead because of sin, but the Spirit is life because of
righteousness. [11] But if the Spirit of Him who
raised Jesus from the dead dwells in you, He who
raised Christ from the dead will also give life to
your mortal bodies through His Spirit who dwells
in you.
[12] Therefore, brethren, we are debtors—not to
the flesh, to live according to the flesh. [13] For if
you live according to the flesh you will die; but if
by the Spirit you put to death the deeds of the body,
you will live. [14] For as many as are led by the
Spirit of God, these are sons of God.*

*(Romans 8:1-14)*

If the house is clean and kept clean, then the
Holy Spirit will manifest Himself in us and He
will tell us of the things of God. He will talk to us
(through our spirits) by His Holy Spirit.

To be indwelt by Him and to remain aware of
His Presence is the only way to be men, husbands,
and fathers who will be able to assume headship
the way God wants us to. The highest goal for
every man should be to be like Jesus

*For whom He foreknew, He also predestined to be
conformed to the image of His Son, that He might
be the firstborn among many brethren.*

*(Romans 8:29)*

He (God) foreknew us and predestined us to be conformed to the image of His Son, that His Son might be the first born among many brethren. We are the many brethren.

We twist God's Word. God said, "Let us make man in our image according to our likeness." We say, "Let us make God in our image according to our likeness." That will not work.

How do we become real men? How do we become good husbands? How do we become good fathers? How do we get to live out headship in our homes? How do we become more Christlike? By saturating ourselves with the Word of God. The more of His Word we have in us, the quicker we will reach these goals.

We are three-dimensional; body, soul and spirit. We feed our bodies every day. We wash them, groom them, feed them good food, rest them, exercise them, all so that they will stay healthy and fit. We take care of our souls (our minds, our wills and our emotions), every day. We read , write, talk, listen, and rest. Our spirits need the same care. They need to be fed every day. There should never be a day that we fail to take time to be alone with God, to pray and to study His Word. The Bible tells us to "be sober, be vigilant, because your adversary the devil walks about like a roaring lion, seeking whom he may devour." (1Peter 5:8) Don't drop your guard. Satan wants us to give in to the things of the flesh. That is his mission, and he will hit us wherever he can.

We have seen in the Word how God created man, and how He created woman. We have seen how He made us in different ways and gave us different roles. We've learned that we need to identify these roles and separate them in order for us to function as the kind of men God wants us to be. Hopefully we have a pretty clear picture of how the world has perverted manhood and reduced us to a generation of wimps. We can all agree that the highest measure of manhood is to be like Jesus. We see how He came and established His Church and how He governs it, guides, it and loves it. We want to be men like Jesus, to be the head as Jesus is, to be the husbands that love our wives the way Jesus loves His Church. In order to do this, we have to take a hard look at ourselves. We must look into our hearts and be willing to change. We have to be willing to let go of the world's way and to fill our hearts with the things of God. We have to cleanse the temple of the plagued stones. We also looked at how to love, how to be a husband, how to be a parent, how to walk in headship, and how to make it work, all based on the Word of

God. You might agree with all of it, some of it, or none of it. That is up to you!

I want to emphasize that the answers for us men do not lie in a weekly visit to a church, a marriage workshop, a week-end retreat, reading a book or even in reading the Bible itself. These things are our helps, to edify and to encourage us towards the real answer which is:

100% Commitment to God.
100% Commitment to prayer.
100% Commitment to abiding in Him.

*"I am the true vine, and My Father is the vinedresser. [2] Every branch in Me that does not bear fruit He takes away; and every branch that bears fruit He prunes, that it may bear more fruit. [3] You are already clean because of the word which I have spoken to you. [4] **Abide** in Me, and I in you. As the branch cannot bear fruit of itself, unless it **abides** in the vine, neither can you, unless you **abide** in Me. [5] I am the vine, you are the branches. He who **abides** in Me, and I in him, bears much fruit; for without Me you can do nothing. [6] If anyone does not **abide** in Me, he is cast out as a branch and is withered; and they gather them and throw them into the fire, and they are burned. [7] If you **abide** in Me, and My words **abide** in you, you will ask what you desire, and it shall be done for you. [8] By this My Father is glorified, that you bear much fruit; so you will be My disciples.*

*[9] "As the Father loved Me, I also have loved you; **abide** in My love. [10] If you keep My commandments, you will **abide** in My love, just as I have kept My Father's commandments and **abide** in His love. [11] These things I have spoken to you, that My joy may remain in you, and that your joy may be full. [12] This is My commandment, that you love one another as I have loved you.*

*(John 15:1-12)*

The word **"abide"** means: "to dwell, rest, continue, stand firm, or be stationary for anytime indefinitely. To continue permanently or in the same state; to be firm and immovable; to remain; to wait for; to be prepared for; to endure." (Webster's 1828)

I have been told by many, that I am a bottom-line type of guy. I remember a bumper sticker that was printed shortly after I made my commitment to the Lord. It said, "God said it; I believe it; that settles it." That remained imbedded in my mind all these years. John 15, verses 1-10 to me bottom-lines our whole Christian walk. The   following words are very important for us to understand. **Without Me (*Jesus*) you can do nothing, but if you will abide (*dwell, rest, continue, wait, endure etc.*) in Me, then whatever you *desire* and ask for *shall* be *done for you*.** Then, in verse 12 Jesus bottom-lines it further by commanding us

**"to love one another as He has loved us."** God's Word is true. There isn't anything that is above it. The scripture says that he magnifies His Word above His name.(Psalm 138:2) There never has been anything written that has survived the test of time like the Bible.

There is nothing like this Christian walk. **There just is nothing like it.** When you are sold out to the Lord and you obey Him and trust Him, ignoring the circumstances, believing **He will do what He says He will do**, then life takes on new meaning, one of love, joy and peace.

It is said that there are an estimated 3600 promises in the Bible. I would like to receive as many of these promises as I can.

> *But without faith it is impossible to please Him, for he who comes to God must believe that He is, and that He is a rewarder of those who diligently seek Him.*
>
> *(Hebrews 11:6)*

"Diligently" means - "with steady application and care: not carelessly." (Webster's 1828)

> *I can do all things through Christ who strengthens me.*
>
> *(Phillipians 4:13)*

In Him and only in Him will we find success in life: In our manhood, in our marriage, in our emotions, in our jobs, with our children. Nothing else works: Not riches, nor fame, nor drugs, nor alcohol, nor sex. **NOTHING BUT JESUS.**

2000 years ago, Jesus asked Peter and the other disciples this question, and it is recorded in Matthew 16:15, "But who do you say that I am?" Peter said, "You are the Christ", (meaning the anointed one, the Messiah, the Savior), "the Son of the living God." Later on Peter told Jesus "I will **die** for you." (Matthew 26:35) Jesus knew Peter would **die** for Him. He knows we would **die** for Him. But, that is not what He was asking of Peter or of us. What He was asking then and still is asking today is;

Peter, will you **live** for Me?
Walter, will you **live** for Me?
_____, will you **live** for Me?
**AMEN**

# Epilogue

If someone tells you that this book will help you in your marriage, but you have never committed your life to the Lord Jesus, it probably will not be of much benefit to you.

Jesus said in John 3:3"... unless one is born again, he cannot see the kingdom of God." Nicodemus who was a Pharisee (they were the religious people of that time) couldn't understand that. He questioned what it meant. People today are still questioning what that phrase "Born Again" means. It is not always very well accepted. Maybe in our zeal to share our new found joy, we Christians have offended people with our do's and don'ts and our religious approach to sharing the Gospel of Jesus Christ.

*Jesus* is the one who said, "You must be born again." Often we look at the kingdom of God as something for the future. But it is not! It is for now! It is so simple. If you want to walk in the fullness of God, if you want to be assured of eternal life with Him, forever and ever, if you want to enjoy all He has for you on earth, if you want to understand the things of the Spirit, if you want to be the kind of man you were created to be, if you want to walk in love and joy and peace, if you have the "Want-To," then you must invite Jesus into your heart and become "born again." When you do that and mean it from your heart, life takes on a whole new meaning. You become a new person.

*Therefore, if anyone is in Christ, he is a new creation; old things have passed away; behold all things have become new.*

*(2 Corinthians 5:17)*

The Bible says we must acknowledge the fact that we are sinners, (Romans 3:23); We must repent of our sins, (Luke 13:3); We must confess with our mouth the Lord Jesus, (Romans 10:9); we must forsake our wicked ways, (Isaiah 55:7); We must believe, (Mark 16:6); We must receive, (John 1:11-12).

Why not do that now? You will be on the way to seeing the kingdom of God. If you can say the following prayer from your heart, you too will be born again:

**"Salvation Prayer."**

**Lord Jesus, I know I am a sinner. I am sorry for all my sins and I ask your forgiveness. I know that you died for my sins and that God raised you from the dead. I forsake satan and all his evil works. I receive you now as my personal Savior and invite You to manage my life. Come, live in my heart, Lord Jesus, so I can live my life for You. Amen.**

*If the foundations are destroyed, What can
the righteous do? (Psalm 11:3)*

The following is a quote taken from the preface of Noah Webster's 1828 American Dictionary. Published by Foundation for American Christian Education San Francisco, California.

"Noah Webster's 1828 American Dictionary of the English Language was produced during the years when the American home, church and school were established upon a Biblical and a patriotic basis. It contains the greatest number of Biblical definitions given in any secular volume. Webster considered education 'useless without the Bible.'

Today when the Biblical basis of education is under systematic attack we need to capitalize upon the availability of our first American dictionary — the only dictionary in the world to 'draw water out of the wells of salvation' — to utilize God's written word as a key to the meaning of words. Historically, it documents the degree to which the Bible was America's basic text book in all fields."

# Book Order Form

**Genevieve M. White**
**56 Lisa Street**
**Plymouth, MA 02360**
**617-288-6140**

Please send me _____ copies of *Daughters of Sarah* by Genevieve M. White, at the rate of $12.00 each, plus shipping charges noted below, for one to nine copies.

Please send me _____ copies of *Beyond Daughters of Sarah* by Genevieve M. White, at the rate of $12.00 each, plus shipping charges noted below, for one to nine copies.

Please send me _____ copies of *Freedom for Daughters of Sarah* by Genevieve M. White, at the rate of $12.00 each, plus shipping charges noted below, for one to nine copies.

Please send me _____ copies of *Sons of Abraham* by Walter F. White, at the rate of $12.00 each, plus shipping charges noted below, for one to nine copies.

Delivery is free within the U.S.A. on orders of ten or more copies to the same address.

**You may order any combination of these titles to earn the reduced or free shipping charges.**

Note: Please call for bookstore rates on 25 or more books.

Name _____

Address _____

City _____ State _____ Zip_____

## Shipping Charges

| Quantity of Books | Shipping Charge |
|---|---|
| 1 | $6.00 |
| 2-3 | $7.00 |
| 4-6 | $8.00 |
| 7-9 | $9.00 |
| 10-25 | FREE |

*Freedom for Daughters of Sarah* is just that! An experience of freedom through reading the powerful testimonies from around the world that reflect the changes that the Word of God and the power of the Holy Spirit can make in a person's life when they penetrate the hearts of those open to receive. The book is also a witness to the seeds planted and the fruit produced through *Daughters of Sarah, Sons of Abraham* and *Beyond Daughters of Sarah*.

*Daughters of Sarah* – This is a book of hope and encouragement. On first reading it will relieve the wife of the indecision regarding God's will for her life and will give her firm and immediate direction. It will also be a very real help to those who are separated or divorced or just not experiencing the joy and fullness God planned when He created marriage. Answers to some very tough questions are dealt with in this book. Also, there are powerful testimonies of how God moves when women choose to obey him.

**Elisabeth Elliot** wrote, *What an encouragement to find another author "on my wavelength"! You and I have been reading the same Book! Thank you for sending yours–in line with Scripture, thank God. I had just answered a letter from a lady who wrote, "My husband is not a Christian and I'm NOT ABOUT TO SUBMIT TO HIM!!!" So I added a note recommending your book.*

*Sons of Abraham* – by Walter F. White who went to his eternal reward in 2002. This book clearly defines a man's role in relation to God, his wife, their children and their children's children. Walter wrote "God's plan for us does not need to be adjusted by the world. It is perfect and works perfectly if we are willing to walk in it, in obedience to His Word." This book is written for men who believe God's Word and want to learn how to walk in the fullness of it. Man was created by God and *He* gave *him* the role as the head of the family.

*Beyond Daughters of Sarah* – This book was written as a follow up to *Daughters of Sarah*. It is especially directed to those of you who have already grasped the truth of God's Word regarding the principles of submission and authority and have begun to walk in this truth. You experienced joy and fulfillment in your marriage. Then came the trials and tribulations and challenges. What did you do? Did you slip into *false* submission? Jesus through His Word will show where you have been deceived. You will be led back to experiencing the peace and love and joy that true submission to God through your husband produces. This book is rich with the Word and you will find yourself receiving blessings, revelation and answers to your prayers.

# Book Order Form

**Genevieve M. White**
**17 Charlemont St.**
**Dorchester, MA 02122**
**617-288-6140**

Please send me _____ copies of *Daughters of Sarah* by Genevieve M. White, at the rate of $12.00 each, plus shipping charges noted below, for one to nine copies.

Please send me _____ copies of *Beyond Daughters of Sarah* by Genevieve M. White, at the rate of $12.00 each, plus shipping charges noted below, for one to nine copies.

Please send me _____ copies of *Freedom for Daughters of Sarah* by Genevieve M. White, at the rate of $12.00 each, plus shipping charges noted below, for one to nine copies.

Please send me _____ copies of *Sons of Abraham* by Walter F. White, at the rate of $12.00 each, plus shipping charges noted below, for one to nine copies.

Delivery is free within the U.S.A. on orders of ten or more copies to the same address.

**You may order any combination of these titles to earn the reduced or free shipping charges.**

Note: Please call for bookstore rates on 25 or more books.

Name _____

Address _____

City _____ State _____ Zip_____

## Shipping Charges

| Quantity of Books | Shipping Charge |
| --- | --- |
| 1 | $6.00 |
| 2-3 | $7.00 |
| 4-6 | $8.00 |
| 7-9 | $9.00 |
| 10-25 | FREE |